Sane New World

Arriving in Britain from the United States in 1977, Ruby Wax began her acting career with the Royal Shakespeare Company. She went on to write and perform in her own hugely popular television programmes for the BBC and Channel 4 and was Script Editor on all series of *Absolutely Fabulous*. Recently she has obtained a Masters degree in Mindfulness-based Cognitive Therapy from Oxford University and spoke at TED Global. She has become the poster girl for mental illness in the UK.

RUBY WAX

Sane New World

Taming the Mind

HODDER

First published in Great Britain in 2013 by Hodder & Stoughton
An Hachette UK company

First published in paperback in 2014

10

A CIP catalogue record for this title is available from the British Library

ISBN 978 1 444 75575 6

Printed and bound by CPI Group (UK) Ltd, Croydon, CR0 4YY

Hodder & Stoughton policy is to use papers that are natural, renewable
and recyclable products and made from wood grown in sustainable
forests. The logging and manufacturing processes are expected to
conform to the environmental regulations of the country of origin. .

Hodder & Stoughton Ltd
338 Euston Road
London NW1 3BH

www.hodder.co.uk

To Ed, Max, Marina and Maddy

Contents

The Beginning

This book is dedicated to my mind, which at one point left town, and to the rest of humanity, who perhaps at one time or another might have misplaced theirs. Though I personally have gone on a rollercoaster ride of depression for most of my adult life, this book is not exclusively for the depressed. I am one of the one in four who has mentally unravelled; this book is for the four in four. It's for everyone, because we all share the same equipment: we suffer, we laugh, we rage, we bitch, we're all vulnerable, delicate creatures under our tough fronts.

In this book I am going to attempt to give a rough guide for where we (the human race) are at right now and offer some suggestions that might make our time on Earth a more joyful experience. I'm not talking 'everyone in the jacuzzi' joyful, I'm talking about the almost blissful state you some-times have when time stops, your body feels like it's home and the volume of those internal critics in your mind lowers. I know those voices well and so many people I meet recognize this dictator barking orders in their minds, keeping them up at night with that tormenting 'I should have, I could have' tape playing relentlessly.

Many of us suffer from the pressures in today's world that drive us from burnout to depression. We are slaves to our busy-ness with an insatiable drive for money, fame, more tweets – you name it, we want it. The problem is, it's only in the last 50 to 100 years that humans have lived with such abundance. We've gone from scarcity (when we were probably somewhat normal and had appetites to match) to the limitless demands we have today. You could say that multi-tasking has driven us mad; like leaving too many windows open on your computer, eventually it will crash. We are simply not equipped for the 21st century. It's too hard, too fast, it's too full of fear; we just don't have the bandwidth. Evolution did not prepare us for this. It's hard enough to keep up with who's bombing whom, so we have no room to understand our emotional landscapes; our hearts bleed because we hear of a beached whale while the next minute we're baying for the blood of someone who stole the last shopping trolley.

The reason I decided to devote myself to this inward journey is because I wanted to find some shelter from the constant hurricanes of depression, which left me depleted and broken. Each episode got longer and deeper. I don't want to blame my parents but childrearing was not their specialty. Friends would come over and there my mother would be, perched on the lampshade, a vulture with a Viennese accent, waiting for someone to drop a crumb. When they did, she would swoop across the room screaming, 'Who brings cookies into a building?' Everyone would run away terrified. It got much, much darker later but I am not going to talk about that here. My point is that this is the type of background that usually leads to a career as a comedian or a serial killer; I went for the comedy.

So, after some serious breakdowns, I decided to go back to school to study psychotherapy to figure out exactly what they were charging £80 an hour for. I used to leave my shrink knowing exactly who I was, until I got to the tube station and then I'd forget again. Also, as I knew nothing about psychology, therapists could tell me anything, so how could I tell if they were any good? Once, when I was on the couch, I caught the shrink behind me eating a pastrami sandwich, mustard all over his face.

So I went to study psychotherapy. I got a library card and never discussed my previous life again. I thought, 'Let's give something back to the world' (I probably didn't but it's a good line). I've noticed that many women like myself choose to study therapy when they meet the wild surf of menopause; the hormones dry up and they realize the chances are low they're ever going to be hit on again, so they find themselves wanting to care for other people or starting a rest home for stray cats.

A few years later, I decided to go further and learn about what I was really interested in: the brain. My thinking was, if I learnt how my own engine worked it might prevent me getting stuck in the middle of nowhere, shrieking for someone to come and fix me; I would provide my own AA service. I'd be able to lasso this wild beast of a brain, stop it from churning away over the same ground, keeping me up at nights; worrying, rehashing, regretting and resenting.

After much research, I thought mindfulness might help me best as I had heard it gives you the ability to regulate your own mind. (I would say it saved my life but I'll get to that later in the book.) I decided to go straight to the horse's mouth, to one of the founders of mindfulness-based cognitive therapy, Professor Mark Williams, who told me that unfortunately I would have to get into Oxford University in order to study it alongside neuroscience.

I scraped together some old school records and managed to excavate my one or two decent high school grades, but most of all I give great interview, so I got into that masters course. The other 14 students in my class were very brilliant and looked at me on day one as if they were having an encounter with a third kind; but God dammit, I was there.

So after many decades of agonizing investigation, a masters in mindfulness, a degree in psychotherapy and even a small taste of fame, here I am writing this manual on how to tame your mind.

I'll go into detail later but I want to mention one fact right away; the gold at the end of the rainbow is that YOU CAN CHANGE YOUR MIND AND HOW YOU THINK. This is called neuroplasticity. Your genes, hormones, regions in the brain and early learning do not necessarily determine your fate.

Scientific evidence has shown that neurons (brain cells) can rewire and change patterns throughout your lifetime as a result of your experiences and how you think about them. So your thoughts affect the physiology of your brain and the physiology affects your thoughts.

Think about sex for a minute. That's Ok, I'll wait. Once you get an inkling, a whole cascade of hormones is let loose in your body to get you ready to cha-cha. Sometimes it's the other way around; you're minding your own business, for no reason a hormone switches on in your brain and suddenly your thinking goes X-rated.

When your mind changes, your brain changes and because our brains are so malleable, the sky's the limit. I remind you that I got into Oxford in my 50s even though I failed to get a diploma from Busy Beaver nursery school (look it up, that was the actual name) proving really anything is possible. But it takes time to alter your habits of thinking; it won't happen with a weekend workshop on 'How to Tickle Your Inner Angel'. It takes intentional concentration and repetition over time. You can change but only if you make the effort not to do the same old thing, the same old way, day in and day out. You, and the way you see the world, are the architect of how your brain is mapped. This is what scientists are giving us in the 21st century; way beyond what Psychic Madge can read in your palm.

The brain is like a pliable three-pound piece of play-dough; you can re-sculpt it by breaking old mental habits and creating new, more flexible ways of thinking. Gloria Gaynor was wrong when she sang, 'I am what I am'. She will have to change those lyrics but it won't be so easy to dance to. What rhymes with neuroplasticity?

The Inner You

If you can look inside your brain and roughly understand where everything is and how it operates, you might not be able to completely know yourself but with practice you may be able to fix yourself. Learning how to self-regulate means you can sense the early warnings before a full-on burnout or depression and do something about it. So much is known about this idea of self-regulation; it may (and I hope it does) shortly become the buzzword of this decade. We can, with certain practices such as mindfulness, actually have some control over the chemicals in our brains that drive us to stress, to anxiety and even to happiness. This remarkable organ in our heads holds infinite wisdom but so few of us know how to use it. It's similar to having a Ferrari except no one gave you the keys.

The reality is that the demanding voice in our heads is not who we are, it plays a very small part in the big scheme of things. What's really running you is a million, trillion gigabyte-powered engine room in your brain, managed by your DNA, that instructs hormones, memories, muscles, blood, organs and really everything that happens inside you to ensure that you survive at all costs, and not that stupid inner monologue about why you're too fat to wear tights.

My aim in this book is to show you how to become the master of your mind and not the slave. If you learn how to self-regulate your moods, emotions and thoughts, and focus your mind on what you want to pay attention to rather than be dragged into distraction, you might just reach that illusive thing called happiness. We all have it we just don't know where the 'on' button is. The organ that allows you to realize the world understands so little about itself.

(Yes Oprah, I'm available.)

Why We Need a Manual

What is our point on Earth? Everyone wants to know. So the question is not, 'To be or not to be?' The big questions are, 'What are we meant to be doing while we're being?' and 'How do I run and manage this thing called "me"?'

Our primary problem as a species (I leave out those with religious beliefs – they have their own books) is we have no manual, no instructions that tell us how to live our lives. Domestic appliances have instruction manuals; not us. We're born with absolutely no information, and are reliant on Mommy and Daddy who jam their USB sticks into our innocent hard drives and download their neuroses into us. As I think we've agreed, we're all missing a manual, so I've tried to keep it simple.

Part 1: What's Wrong With Us? For the Normal-Mad

In this part of the guidebook I will examine why we are all in the 'flying by the seat of our pants' school of thought when it comes to living our lives. We assume the next person knows what they're doing; they don't.

Part 2: What's Wrong With Us? For the Mad-Mad

For the depressed, anxious, panic-attacked, OCD'd, over-eaters, drinkers, shoppers, compulsive list-makers, etc. The list is endless.

Part 3: What's in Your Brain/What's on Your Mind?

I will familiarize you with your ingredients: the hormones, neurons, hemispheres, regions etc. so that in Part 4 you'll be able to understand what physically happens in your brain when you practise mindfulness; how it can enhance positive feelings, which ultimately bring happiness.

You are your own cookbook. How you work your brain determines if you're going to become filet mignon or an old kebab.

Part 4: Mindfulness – Taming Your Mind

Think of this part as *Wisdom for Dummies*. I'll show you how to be able to self-regulate your thoughts and emotions to make you the *master* and not the *slave* of your mind.

Part 5: Alternative Suggestions for Peace of Mind

I would never want to be considered evangelical so if mindfulness isn't for you, I'll give you alternative practices that can change your brain.

I hope this book helps you let go of the image you have of yourself if it's getting in your way; I hope I can encourage you to be brave and know that nothing is certain: life flows, changes and ends. Get over your fear. The only way to find any peace is to let it all go and jump into the unknown. Just jump.

Part One

What's Wrong With Us?
For the Normal-Mad

What Drives Us Crazy

There may be many observations in this part that do not resonate with you but we only see the world through our own eyes. I know there are people out there who don't see the world as I do but sadly they aren't writing this book. So if anyone does not suffer from what follows, I apologize if it seems I'm painting the whole human race with the same pessimistic brush. I have reached these conclusions only because everyone I have ever met has complained that these are the areas of life that drive them crazy. I know from the bottom of my heart, they are what drive me crazy.

Critical Voices

Why are we so mean to ourselves? What did we do wrong? Why, if we are the best that evolution has tossed up so far, are we so abusive to ourselves? Each of us has a nagging parent implanted in our heads: 'Don't do that . . . why didn't you . . . you should have . . . but you didn't', on an endless tape. (My mother would say she was only telling me what a failure I was because she loved me.) If most of us ever compared our inner leitmotif, we would sue each other for plagiarism, as our internal themes are so alike.

No other species is as cruel as we are to ourselves. We'd never dream of treating our pets the way we treat ourselves. We whip ourselves to keep moving like we would an old horse, until it falls over exhausted; the hooves made into glue. I have asked so many people if they have ever had a voice in their head that says, 'Congratulations you've done a wonderful job and may I say how attractive you look today'. The answer is no one. I'm sure they're out there, I just never met them.

Once you get an attack of this self-immolation, you're on the slippery slope to a very unhappy state. Your brain just churns away chewing over a problem like a piece of meat that won't go down. There will never be a solution to 'I should have' so you attack, guess who? You. This is why one in four of us is mentally ill.

It's not our fault that we're slave drivers to ourselves because biologically we all have this inbuilt chip that compels us to achieve and move forward. Before we even had words, we had an innate drive in every cell of our body to press on. (Google 'selfish gene'.) All organisms, even worms, have this. It is how one cell becomes two, and two becomes three (I could go on but I haven't got time). Cells keep advancing to the trillion cells that finally make up us. We strive to achieve. The problem is that now we use words and when we don't 'cut the mustard' in our own eyes (which would really hurt) the inner voices begin: 'I should have' and 'I could have'. That old familiar tune.

All of us internalize the voices in our heads from our parents, who probably meant well, but these sentiments stay in there for a lifetime. It's because most parents want to protect their children that you get an abundance of 'you shouldn't . . . you should have', otherwise the child might put his finger in a light socket and be electrocuted. These corrective voices helped you survive as a child; later in life they can either drive you mad with their constant corrections and instructions or they can help you successfully navigate obstacles throughout your life, giving you a smoother ride.

There are parents who encourage their children with positive reinforcement and calming encouragement: 'That's right sweetheart, you did so well, why don't we try it again and you'll be even better?' These children, later in life, may see a close friend passing by who doesn't acknowledge them and their inner voice says, 'Oh, too bad, Fiona must be preoccupied and she looks so lovely, I'll call her later'. Those of us with parents trained by the Gestapo-school-of-child-rearing would react to this incident with, 'Fiona hates my guts, that's why she's ignoring me. She found out I'm a moron, which I am.'

My Story

In my case, I would say the voices were somewhat harsh for a baby; they were less like suggestions and more like commando orders. My mother had a fear of dust so she'd have a sponge in each hand and two stuck to her knees (my mother was completely absorbent) and she'd crawl around behind me on all fours screaming, 'Who brings footprints into a building? Are they criminally insane?' She probably wanted to protect me, from what I don't know, but I was hermetically sealed in my house as a child; everything was wrapped in plastic including my father, grandmother and the dog. Both my parents had to escape Nazi Austria in a laundry basket, just before 'last orders' was shouted and the borders shut down so no one could leave the Fatherland. This probably is what made her so unconsciously fearful, which she projected onto dust balls. (They're easier to blow away.) Whatever the case, I picked up the panic in her voice and that sound has never left my head. So even though I'm not in Nazi Austria, the voices in my head are. Not anyone's fault.

The Search for Happiness

We are all looking for happiness (unless of course we've already got it and blessed are those few that have). This is why we have so many self-help books – enough now to cover the equator 78 times. Have you read *The Secret*? I didn't read it but I know 80 million copies were sold. I did read page one, which informs you that 'the secret' was handed down to us by the ancient Babylonians and clearly it worked for them; that's why there's so many running around, you can't move for all the Babylonians living in London. Next, the author tells you that Plato, Leonardo da Vinci, Beethoven and Einstein were inspired by this book. I'm going to use that idea and give myself reviews from dead people. Apparently the next 200 pages are filled with advice that boils down to, 'Think happy thoughts and your dreams will come true, just like Tinker Bell promised'. (I'm sorry to all you *The Secret* fans, I'm just very bitter about the 80 million copies sold. You can understand.)

All of this self-help was stolen from Walt Disney; he was the father of the New Age. 'Whistle a happy tune; if you believe in fairies, clap your hands.' From this philosophy flowed *The Little Mermaid*, *Snow White* and some early *Mickey Mouse*. Walt knew the secret of happiness. Too bad he's on ice; we've got to defrost this guy to squeeze out some more wisdom. Walt knew when to make an exit.

Staying Busy

This is a method we have devised in order to distract ourselves from the bigger, deeper questions; we have an obsession to keep busy. There is no time to rest and no time to think about what we really should be doing in our limited time on Earth. I'm not criticizing; I'm as driven as the next person. It almost got to the point where I went into labour while doing a TV show. The floor manager gave me '5-4-3-2', someone cut the cord and yelled, 'Action'.

Gandhi said, 'There is more to life than speed'. Unfortunately he didn't tell us what, he just left us hanging while he pranced around in his nappy.

To compensate for this undercurrent of uselessness, we pretend we're all terribly important and that we have something to bring to the world. That's why we have Twitter so we can check how many followers we've got. We can count them; 100, 1000 people you've never met, telling you what they had for lunch, now knowing you exist. That's how we see if we matter. We're like little birds, newly hatched from our eggs going, 'Tweet, tweet, tweet', looking for a little attention, a little love, maybe even a worm – anything will do as long as they notice we're here.

In reality we're all as disposable as wax figures. Once you lose your job or beauty or status, which you will eventually, they melt you down and use you to make the next important person. I went to Madame Tussaud's and there was Charlie Chaplin next to the loo while Nicole Kidman was melted down and made into 150 candles; an icon one minute, a candle the next. Jerry Hall must be on some birthday cake somewhere.

We run because we don't want to look inside and see that there might not be anything there and that searching for meaning is a waste of airtime. We stay busy so we don't have to think about how futile the running is; like dung beetles building a house made of manure, they don't stop and think, 'Hey, where's this going?'

When I have a day off and wake up, I jolt up from the pillow, panicking that I may have nothing of any importance to do. Maybe this is why I, and people I know like me, have to keep busy compiling an endless 'Things to Do' list. For us, busy-ness is our God, we worship busy-ness. People ask me if I'm busy, I tell them, 'I'm so busy I've had two heart attacks'. They congratulate me on this achievement.

We hold those who are on the tightest of schedules in reverence; the busier you are, the higher your status as a human being. For those of us who suffer from this phenom-enon, we have sped up to such a frenzy of things 'to do,' we make ourselves ill just to avoid having to look inside and see that we might not have any point at all. So who is ultimately the winner? The busy, running people? Or maybe it's someone who sits on a rock and fishes all day or someone who has the time to feel the breeze on his face? Who is the real winner? Please, dear God, I hope it's not the guy with the fish.

Here are some common answers to the question, 'Are you busy?'

'I am run off my feet.'
    (Let's picture it, someone somewhere was dashing at

**such a rate he/she literally cracked at the ankle and
just kept going.)**

'I don't know if I'm coming or going.'
   **(Someone once opened a door and just stayed there
for the next five years trying to figure, 'in or out?')**

If you have used either of these responses then you probably
are an A-list person who is 'living the life' even though you
are too busy to have one.

There are women in my neighbourhood in London who
have nothing to do for a living and they are booked to the
hilt. They do Pilates five times a week so they can make their
pelvic floor strong enough to lift the carpet. Dyson could use
them as hoovers. Then they'll shop with their personal shopper
(that takes up a few hours), have their hair blow-dried (that's
another hour), lunch (that's a four-hour filler). Then they
have to pick up the kids, do their homework for them and
then it's time to get ready and go off to attend a charity event.
You know what that entails? They go to a really fancy hotel
and pay £2000 a plate to save a tuna.

Never Enough

These Pilates women complain that their husbands work
until midnight and they're left having to get their spawn
into a nursery school that only takes kids whose IQs have
six digits. I have (in vain) tried to tell them that marriage
is a 'negotiated deal'. I've even made them a little flow-chart
so they can get some perspective. I tell them, 'if your husband
is earning more than £150,000 a year, plus bonuses, as the

wife you have no rights. You take care of the house and the kids. You must give him sex whenever and wherever he wants. And you have to stay thin and young till death do you part.

'If your husband is making around £75,000 a year, you still take care of the house and kids but you may bitch about him up to 27 hours a week to your friends. If he does not help on the weekends, you can withhold the sex.

'If he makes below £10,000, you can let the house and kids to go to hell.' That's all for when the husband is making all the money. If the wife is making all the money, say, she's earning £150,000 a year, which is equivalent to £575,000 in 'Man Money', she will still have to do everything because evolution has not given men eyes to see details such as a hoof print on the carpet. But man does have a very important function and that is to stand there and gaze toward the horizon to make sure there are no wildebeests.

Shopping is Our Search for Love

This need to have more is not limited to the wives of foot-ballers or head honchos of big organizations. We all, in our own way, never stop 'wanting', that's why we need 20,000 feet of mall; big steaming mounds of galleria won't be enough to satisfy. The shopping never stops; the label says it all. Our self-esteem drives us to buy a designer handbag that costs the GNP of Croatia which is why people with nothing will spend their last shekel on Dolce and Gabbana or a £300 pair of Nikes. If you have the tattoo of 'CC' on your handbag, you can get a nod of respect from everyone that passes, even though you're homeless. I once saw a tramp in Miami pushing all his belongings in a shopping cart he stole from Bloomingdale's. He was wearing newspaper and had a cap on his head that said, 'Born to Shop'.

What we throw on our back is our new means of identity. People who wear Prada usually hang out with other Praderites and the same with all other brands; people seek their own level, their own tribe. Picture it, a whole gaggle of Guccis at the watering hole and some Primarks eating a carcass.

P.S. Proof of our insanity is that we actually buy Ugg boots. Where in the brain do we feel a need to look like an Eskimo, as if they ever had any fashion sense?

The 'Fix' of Happiness

Some people think to reach a state of joy, you need to dress in sheets for a lifetime with a dot on your head, on top of a mountain. Some wave crystals, eat turf, pray, chant and dance with the wolves. Contentment might even be possible . . . I'm sure it's feasible to sit on a bench and feed a squirrel without getting antsy. But the trouble is, we always want more. We're the A-list of all species so we go for the Golden Chalice: happiness. It had to be a crazy American who said that we all have the right to pursue happiness. That's why you hear them demanding a double latte caramel macchiato every morning with their smiling teeth just before they chirp, 'Have a nice day'. There are some lucky people who feel they experience happiness when they gaze at a cloud or walk on the beach but the rest of us only get that special tingly buzz when we've bought, won, achieved, hooked or booked something. Then our own brains give us a hit of dopamine, which makes us feel good. We don't need substances; we are our own drug dealers.

The problem is, the hit of 'happiness' usually lasts as long as a cigarette so we have to continually search for the next fix. It's as though as a species we have no brakes, only breakdowns. Mother Nature's little joke on us is that the original object of desire isn't so much fun when we get it, so unless we can up the stakes all the time, we can't get that burst of internal fireworks we call happiness. Most animals just eat their fill and walk away but not us, we keep glutting ourselves even though the next bite never tastes as good as the first one.

The Hierarchy of Western Wants (According to Me)

- Food and/or water
- Mattress
- Roof
- House
- Normal car
- Second house
- Pool
- Porsche
- Flying economy class
- Business class
- First class
- Private jet
- Private jet with jacuzzi
- Meeting Oprah

This failure to get what we want leaves us in a state of permanent desire. Magazines understand that they make us salivate for the unobtainable; the chase is better than the kill. People who collect art pay £15 million for some semen on a cracker and then never notice it once it's on their wall. They'll be back licking the pages of Sotheby's catalogue for what they crave next. If we're not wanting, we're waiting. Waiting for what, we don't know, but something and it's going to happen soon. Waiting for our screenplay to be commissioned about a clown who falls in love with a squirrel and then decides to become a car dealer. Waiting for the money to roll in for an idea about inventing soup in a solid form; it's all about to happen next week, next year, we don't mind how long, as long as we're in a suspended state of waiting.

A new phenomenon that arises from our insatiable appetites is the sense of entitlement; now everyone thinks they deserve to be a winner. This is why so many deluded people with absolutely no sense of shame have the audacity to try out for *X Factor* when they have the voice of a toad. Self-help books will tell you that the only thing standing in your way is you. 'You can be beautiful if you think you are', they say. This is why you see the truly self-deluded paint their nails with tiny diamantes embedded in bloodbath-red extensions, as if no one will notice that they are the size of Tibet.

Negative Thinking

Once we humans have the basics for survival, i.e. food, water and mascara, you would think we should be on our knees, kissing the ground in gratitude for our aliveness, for being able to see through our eyes, hear through our ears, and best of all, eat. Let us have a moment's silence to thank the Big Bang for making it possible that eventually we could experience the taste of Ben & Jerry's Chunky Monkey Ice Cream.

But even with all these miracles we still suffer and it's all because of our negative thinking. Animals don't have negative thoughts; they're out there having the time of their lives, swinging from branches, mating with nearly everyone who comes up behind them. And us? We ruminate on things, worry, regret, resent; who picked the short straw, do you think? Most awful of all is that we can project to the future and figure out that we will eventually lose our looks and dare I say it . . . die.

See how there's always a grenade at the bottom of the cookie jar? It's so like the story of my life – whenever I achieve a little something and am complimented, shortly thereafter I am swiftly kicked in the ass by karma. The more you have (looks, money, fame) the more you suffer when you lose it. There is always a bill to pay. Luckily, they bless people like Liza Minnelli with a dollop of unawareness so when they begin to crinkle and melt into oblivion, they're the last to know and they just keep on kickin' those 'hoofers' on ol' Broadway, even though you hear the sound of their arthritic hips cracking in the effort. (This probably sounds judgmental but I get evolved later in the book so just bear with me now.)

Those of us who aren't on the brink of starvation or elimination or living in squalor are condemned to a life of worrying about trivia. It all went downhill when we crawled out of the jungle. We just don't know what to think about next after fulfilling basic needs; so we makeover our kitchens. In my neighbourhood all the surfaces in this year's kitchens are buffed silver metal resembling what you'd find in mortuaries. You're scared to open a drawer in case a toe hangs out with a label dangling from it. Now they are digging down below the kitchens to make more floors until they're hitting volcanic rock. Some have lap pools they will never lap in. I know someone who is building an underground vineyard.

Bathrooms of Grandeur

My theory is you can tell how mentally deranged someone is by viewing their bathroom. If they believe they need a chandelier, an Italian marble tub and a toilet that performs more than three functions (now some of them play Rachmaninoff when you lift the lid and squirt you with lilac perfume after you pee) they are not a well person and have strayed far, far away from sanity. Freud should have come up with a therapy where you interrogate the clients about how they envision the decor of their bathrooms rather than asking about sex. Sex tells you nothing. How you want your lavatory to look is the gateway to the unconscious. A bathroom is a place where you should have no airs or graces because it's just you and it. There is no room in there for narcissism, this is merely a toilet, where you really see yourself for what you are and get a whiff of reality. On the toilet no one is a star. Remember that and you will go far in life.

Our Need to Be Special

Our status used to be based on bloodlines, on whether you were a Princess or a Pea. (See Battle of the Sperm.) Now we determine each other's worth by asking, 'What do you do?' If you say 'nothing', people move away from you as if you're a corpse. Our identity is on our business cards, and new titles emerge every year to define increasingly abstract roles. Job descriptions like 'consultancy' are ambiguous. (If everyone's a consultant, who is left needing one?) These days 'motivational speakers' are also considered big shots. We confuse bravery with bravura. I've seen motivational speakers who are brought in to companies to tell you about rowing across the Atlantic with one arm. How is this helping the company? That person isn't brave, he's nuts. And these speakers are starting to get competitive; apparently someone has claimed he climbed Mount Everest using only his nostrils.

Each of us thinks somewhere inside we have a purpose. Long ago we didn't have this existentialist angst; we were hunters or gatherers. A hunter hunted, a gatherer gathered (Jewish people pointed rather than doing either). Back then there was no such thing as individuality so you couldn't distinguish 'you' from anyone else unless you wore a hat or had more hair but basically we were all the same: grunting and foraging.

In those days you didn't need a manual. You were born, drove an ox around a field, multiplied and died. No one complained; plagues came and went – smallpox, influenza, you name them you had them – and everyone had the same attitude, 'Shit happens'. Now it's an outrage: 'How dare some virus wipe us out? Do they know who we are? We're superior beings, the crème de la crème of all that live and breathe; top of the food chain'.

It all went wrong when some deluded optimist wrote the words, 'All men are created equal'. This is clearly not the case; some people are losers. He never even lived to see the can of worms he released once he wrote that with his feather. He just signed his autograph and let the chaos begin. (I'm going to name names. It was Thomas Jefferson – another American.)

The Big Team – Happy Days

We were at our happiest when we used to drive our yoke-necklaced oxen around a field because then we were all working together as a big tribe, a team. Ok, it was tough but we had some laughs out there in the blizzard conditions. We needed to form tribes in order to fight off neighbouring tribes who tried to steal our oxen. Without an ox you're nothing. After that, the numbers of people in a tribe diminished because along came the gun and then you didn't really need a lot of people, just one guy with a good trigger finger. That's why now we don't have this sense of teamwork; we're all alone hunkering in our corners, clutching our weapons.

The only time we do get a sense of belonging to a tribe is when we're facing a disaster like a hurricane, Godzilla or a war. In the UK the only time everyone unites is when they're reminiscing about the Second World War; when they get fuelled up on the Blitzkrieg spirit, they all start blubbing away singing those 'We'll Meet Again' songs they heard on the wireless. Every Christmas, my husband's parents would dress up as Luftwaffe and RAF pilots and run around the living room going, 'We shall fight them on the beaches!' and screaming, 'We shall never surrender', as they smashed into the TV set.

In my opinion, our downfall began when we started to think of ourselves as 'individuals'. I read somewhere, don't ask me where, that hundreds and hundreds of years ago there was no word for 'I'. There was only the word for 'we'. No one was lonely back then. The trouble started when the individual came into the picture. Remember the wheel? Back millions of years ago when we made the wheel? We don't know who made it. There was no wheel by Chanel. Remember when we all worked together to make fire? We don't know who lit the first match – he was just some guy and he didn't need his name in lights. Now agents and managers have to get involved and skim 20 per cent off the top for just standing there.

Simple animals have all the luck. They're delighted to still work as a team. They're delighted to be part of a gaggle, or flock, or swarm. Goose in the back row of the flying formation? He's proud to be there. He's overjoyed. It's his job in life. Not us anymore. Our earliest instinct is to bond together and socialize; our very DNA gives us instructions on how to mingle. Natural selection is like a beauty contest, no one remembers who came in second. Nature is so cruel: one tiny weakness, a blemish, a flipper instead of an arm and you're out of the running . . . gone.

You know who I blame for all this? Freud. If he hadn't mentioned an ego, we would never have had one. Because of him it's all about me. Me, I need to be the next Kate Moss. Me, I need to run Virgin. Me, I need to be in *Hello* and I'll do anything to get on television. 'You want me to eat my mother-in-law? Toss her on the barbecue.'

So this is the human condition: we're living longer, getting taller, and are a push of a finger away from every other person on the planet and yet we do not know how to run ourselves. Maybe we're not supposed to know and when we're finished filling the world with parking lots, muffin shops and Starbucks, our point on Earth is finished and with one big cataclysmic boom we'll be gone.

Millions of years of natural selection, and this is what we've come to. We want to be the most famous, the richest, the thinnest and the busiest. Darwin would shit himself in the pants.

The Problem with Change

I have given you a taster of the good news already: WE CAN CHANGE. But here I ought to point out, as we are focusing on the problems of living in modern times, that when you do change, those around you won't like it. People will not let go of their image of you, even though you have thoroughly redecorated your inner self. They want you to stay as they remember you so that they feel they aren't changing either, that they are still gloriously youthful. This is why we don't want to see an old movie star because it makes us think of our own mortality. Sometimes they will cast an 'older' woman (in her 50s!) but they'll make sure she dies of something terminal half-way through. No one wants to see an ageing face on the screen, especially in HD. (I once saw myself in HD, I looked like a close-up of an elephant.) We run to doctors to fight off Mr Gravity for another year but it's hopeless. We should tell ourselves, 'The Christmas tree is dead already, stop trying to decorate it with fancy tinsel, it won't help.'

I'm not leaving myself out of this; I give thanks every day to surgeons who have helped me look this pert long after pertness should have died. I'm sure my insides are like the old Dorian Gray, while my face looks all shiny and new. I once said to Jennifer Saunders wasn't it amazing that you couldn't tell I've had any work done on my face? She said that I was delusional and that it was obvious. I will never tell anyone how old I am. The year I was born will never pass these lips without water-boarding. Actually, I don't even remember the year I was born. I set my burglar alarm to remind me. I've had my house robbed many times, the police come over and I can't remember what I set the alarm at: 1971? 1932? 1995? Could be anything.

27

So many people want to label you as funny or aggressive or a mess. We are condemned by other people to stagnate in the image they have of us; held ransom by their expectations like a butterfly pinned on cardboard. I'm still asked by taxi drivers, as if this wouldn't hurt me, why I am no longer on television? In the past, I used to have to choke back the bile as I felt that stab in my heart. I used to answer with, 'Because I have terminal cancer'. That usually shut them up pretty quickish. I stopped doing that because I've learnt that if you let out your anger on someone, it comes back to you like acid reflux and you've poisoned yourself and feel toxic and nause-ated while the taxi driver probably just goes back to his home and wife and has a lovely life.

I had to change, I didn't have a choice as my career in television was pulled out like a rug from under me and I was replaced by a younger (but not as funny) version of me. Anyway I let it go and yes, it's painful at first when no one looks at you. Fame is very addictive and as our spotlight fades, most people are desperate to cling on and we'll do anything. 'Please do a documentary about my gall bladder operation. I'll even play a corpse.'

Eventually it's quite liberating to not be noticed and you rejoin the human race. When you go on the tube and no one recognizes you, it's a wake-up call; you realize how up your own ass you have been and that now it's time to come out and smell the Circle Line. There's a downside to becoming a normal person; when you tell the ticket guy at the exit that you forgot to buy a ticket and you think he'll go, 'Ha ha you're the one from TV', and let you off, you discover that this time he doesn't and he tells you to get a ticket or you'll be arrested.

When I decided to re-invent myself (which we all have to do in life at least five times, because we were meant to be dead by 30) and I went back to school to learn how to be a therapist, my friends said that the clients would think it was a joke. They would expect TV cameras to be following me into the room and either freak out or start auditioning. I was under the impression that the woman (me) who had that job in television was effectively dead.

The point is, we're all changing all the time. You once found it hard to tie a shoelace and now you don't even have to look. The change is so subtle; you think that whatever you feel like right now is how you always felt. Our brain can trick us into thinking life stands still. In the end this causes the human race the most heartache.

Blinkered Vision

As you get older you don't see many things as unique any more. Whatever we experience in the present, we automatically go back through the filofax in our minds to figure out what it reminds us of. We do this for the sake of survival so, say, we have had a bad experience with a man with a moustache, now we don't trust anyone with a moustache. And, because we see everybody through the filter of who they remind us of, whoever we meet is therefore labelled with that image, frozen in ice for all time. We're not aware of how biased our memories make us and how they affect our view of the world.

And as we get older, our lenses get more and more narrow and blurrier until we only see our own tiny pin-point view; this limited vision eventually makes bigots of us all. This is why so many marriages fall apart. You meet someone, think that you know them, marry them and then ten years later you divorce them because they turned out not to be who you thought they were. They never were. I realized many years after I married that I chose my husband because he has the eyebrows of Jeff Bridges. Now, I have to live daily with the disappointment that it's actually him I'm with and not Jeff. God knows who he thought I was.

It goes further. We then unconsciously create situations that back up our beliefs, just to prove our point of view is right. We all know those women who keep dating the same kind of guy just to keep up their image of themselves as 'victim' and to reinforce the fact that 'all men are bastards'. They give you stories about how he seemed so perfect on the 'Serial Killer' website and yet, after leaving a grenade on the pillow, he never called again. Why?

It's amazing how we will suffer pain and abuse to keep our lives predictable. We'll let our inner voices brutalize us, rather than live with the possibility that we might be wrong about how we see things. We'll think, 'Well at least it's a pain that's familiar'.

Uncertainty is our biggest fear so we keep up the idea that our vision of the world is reality. We use our minds to construct a picture of the world, judging it, making sure it fits with our past image of things and then anticipating how our past behaviours might affect the future. We never see the world as it really is but only how we see it. And because we're trapped in our own interpretation, we are prepared to go to war with other people caught in *their* view of reality – and never the twain shall meet. All this is the sound of people embedded in their own lives, believing their reality is the only reality, thinking the things they think matter; it's the sound of solipsism. This could be why the world is in such a bad shape. It is the nub of all our problems and until we realize how limited our views are, we'll never agree on anything. We have to try to see what other people see, through their eyes, only then can we come up with some cohesive resolution. This is my statement on world peace: take it or leave it.

My Story

I don't mind change. I come from a long line of unpredictability as my ancestors didn't stick around for long in any one place. Maybe it's because I'm the daughter of immigrants that I'm always ready to jump ship, to change my location fast in case we're exterminated again. My fellow immigrants don't get sentimental about things like furniture or heirlooms; this is because we're constantly scuttling across borders, fleeing with pianos on our backs.

My fantasy is living in a simple hotel room, with no knick-knacks, only a phone for room service. I never get it when I see people waving their national flag, getting all weepy, singing some dirge about their homeland. Everyone sobbing for the old country (which is just a wet piece of peat moss) going on and on about how many generations back their people lived on this potato farm (said with an Irish accent) and how they loved it even though they've probably emigrated to another country. To me it's dirt, to them it's land: same thing. My people this, my people that. I have no real people except when I was in the mental institution and then it was full of them. They were my people, because they did not answer with 'fine' when you asked how they were. We didn't need a flag.

My career ended with a bang in that I ended up in an asylum. We're always surprised when something ends; everything ends, so why do we never think it's our turn? One of my last interviews was with Ben Stiller who just answered my questions with 'yes' and 'no' and I knew I had a car crash on my hands. Actually the very last interview show I did was with a star (who shall remain nameless) whose publicity agent only allowed me to go shopping with her in her friend's shop where she wandered around saying things like, 'This is nice'. Then we went to her Pilates class where I was allowed to film her doing a sit-up. She finally spoke at the end of the show in a coffee shop and I got a 45-minute speech about politics in Palestine or Panama or Bosnia; it was all my fault, the whole Bush administration was my fault. I knew the show needed some comedy so on the way out of the coffee shop I bought her (only in New York) a plastic donkey into whose behind you could put a lighted cigarette and watch the smoke come out of its mouth. She held it and looked at me as if to say, 'You are lower than a worm'. That was the last time I inter-viewed anyone. As I watched them try to edit in one useable sentence to save the show from the 'Ben Stiller as a corpse' and 'Joan of Arc/nameless star' interviews I knew it was over; I would be bidding a fond farewell to this profession.

On the way down the escalator of showbusiness, I finally hit the basement when I made a double suicide pact with Richard E. Grant by doing a show I hope you missed called *Celebrity Shark Bait*. Here's a clue;

the sharks weren't the celebrities. We did it for the money and a chance to see Cape Town and we put the swimming with great white sharks in the back burner of our minds. Besides us on this show, there was also a girl (forgot name) from some soap (forgot name) who wore very low cut tops to show off her white, milky breasts. They filmed her most days and Richard and I were told they didn't need us, so we told estate agents we were looking for a house to buy and snooped into people's homes. Meanwhile, Milky Breasts was now being filmed (I'm not making this up) in a freezer where they hang dead pigs from hooks all around her while she stood freezing in her bikini. The point of this was to prepare her for the cold water. P.S. We were going to wear dry suits for the dive so there was no point in the pig scene except to see her nipples.

The day came for the shark dive; an obese lesbian gave us instructions on the do's and don'ts of how to behave in the shark cage. The woman, who had 'Shark Lady' printed on her red jacket, told us not to worry as she had been doing this for over 25 years and it was perfectly safe. As she tossed large chunks of tuna into the sea for chumming (getting some blood in the water to attract the great white sharks and drive them into a feeding frenzy) we noticed she only had two fingers. It turns out Milky Breasts wouldn't get in the water – she was too scared – and so Richard and I were lowered down as bait. Suddenly something about 20 feet long glided at us, looked at us with dead eyes and swam away. The shark must have known our television careers were over and went off looking for an A-list celebrity. We became hysterical at the bottom of the cage, I laughed until urine came out of my rubber wet suit collar. Months later we saw the show. We were used as cut-aways to the Breasts and when we were lowered in the cage they dubbed in screaming, thus not only humiliating us but making us look like wimps; two old has-beens sunk in the bottom of a tube. I decided to let go of showbusiness and begin again, slowly weaning myself off fame.

So I'm not nostalgic about leaving things. As far as my career or my university or my hometown went, I was on the bus out of town at the right time because I knew to walk away before I was pushed out. I never wanted to be the last one to leave the party. If you don't move on, you get stuck and it becomes pathetic when you're left clutching onto your past, remembering your school days, singing the old songs and boring everyone to death. The ultimate freedom lies in knowing everything, including you, is in a state of flux; you're never still, you're always 'nexting'; billions of your cells are born, billions die. In seven years you will be a whole new version of you and the old you, a pile of dandruff flakes.

Have We Overloaded?
How Much Should We Know?

Our little brains are on a daily drip-feed of everything from fashion tips to traffic updates to terrorist attacks. Is there a limit? I'd like to know. I wish there was some kind of service that tells you how much your particular mind can take. What is your capacity? When is there too much information to hold in one head? Why can't those of us filled to capacity hold up our hand and say, 'I can take no more, please don't tell me anything else'? I can only retain my Visa number. I cannot also remember my password for PayPal and Twitter, my brain floweth over. I had my brain tested a few months ago by a psychologist and he said that I had very little ram space so I can only hold about three numbers at once and I can't build an argument because I forget where I started. I have other problems with numbers. I once called my husband from South Africa and told him I'd got a house for a steal, for 10,000 rand (£1000). I was three decimals off: it was 10 million (£100,000).

How much information are we supposed to be able to take in? I'm sure we're only equipped to know what's happening on our street and maybe the local deli, but if there's a 3.6 earthquake in Kow Loo Toik, do I have to know? If the islands off Papua New Guinea flood, what am I supposed to do? Fly over there; get in a canoe with a hand pump and start draining? Ok, if you show me a photo of a maimed person, I will write you a cheque immediately, but most of the time what are we supposed to feel about these global disasters? I would probably like to know if my next-door neighbour gets shot but maybe I'm not so upset if it's someone three blocks away. How close am I to the bullets? That's what I want to know. I feel terrible saying this but it's what I'm thinking.

When there was a hurricane in New York, there were huge headlines and 240 photos of every drop of rain, wet people being interviewed, for their first smell of fame (you can see a glint in the eye) aware they will be seen all over the world as they said something so original: 'I was in my house and I heard wind and I ran out of my house'. New Yorkers were crying, screaming, kvetching (that's what Jews do) that their cars stalled, their hair was blown off. Yet, at the same time, Haiti was nearly devastated; 66 people died and hardly a flicker of coverage. You saw some black people wading in some water but no close-ups.

I'm sceptical as to why people need to know about worldwide atrocities. I know people who watch CNN all day, particularly when working out on the StairMaster, buffing their butts while those headlines of disaster slap them in the face with an up-to-the-minute report on another high school shooting. You can see a lip-lubed anchor woman running over to an injured cheerleader, shoving the microphone in her face demanding, 'How do you feel about the incident?' giving her a little kick as she sinks into unconsciousness. 'How do you feel?' She has the look of a cat before it kills a mouse as she turns to the camera and says, 'Well, Jerry, that's all on the up-to-the-minute report on the tragedy happening down here, back to you.'

In some deep, dark way we all become salacious around a disaster; our mouths water slightly when there's a real emergency. Hurricanes, typhoons, wars, shootings, epidemics; we're a little aroused because now we really have something to think about rather than our monotonous lives; something to take the focus away from our to-do list. We have a little break to think, 'Well thank God it's not me'. Then we forget again after a few days and get on with worrying about the pick-up at the dry cleaner and buying another light bulb. You can see the look of disappointment on people's faces when the report comes that the hurricane has dipped from 3000 knots to a light breeze. We all love a disaster; nothing tastes as good. The savage still lurks underneath no matter what we're wearing.

We the Emotionally Inept

We have created rockets to the moon, computers that can . . . well, you name it, they can do it and Starbucks on every corner of the world, but the other part of us, the emotional bit, is still wearing nappies. Emotionally we are on all fours, grazing our knuckles on the ground, looking out naively from under our one big eyebrow. Many of us don't even like to say the 'E' word (emotion) because some of us think it is a glitch in this otherwise perfect human machine. Emotions are to be eradicated as quickly as possible like a blemish or a laugh line.

But it is these lurking emotions that cause us the most trouble and we haven't risen above them. We're still slaves to them when they rear their ugly heads.

We used to hold in high esteem those who got the highest grades at school and they went on to be hugely successful. (Times have changed. There's not some little guy at the top selling soap powder any more, now you need an MBA from Harvard just to put on your pants.) We've learnt that the brightest might be the very ones who screw us the hardest. They know the math; they feel they can rob the bank. We used to trust these guys, we thought they were like Superman. To relax on weekends they go helicopter skiing in Alaska, not just a double black run for them, they have to leap from a plane. To unwind, I chew a chicken bone in front of the television; they jump down a cliff.

Want my advice? If you're checking out whom you want to do business with, ask what they do to relax on the weekends. If they say helicopter skiing, walk away, they are mentally not right. The most cognitively brilliant people usually have had to sacrifice their emotional selves. They live in a fog of facts rarely creating a new one, just regurgitating everything they've ever learnt and we're supposed to think that's smart. That's a walking Wikipedia not a human being. This also might mean they're not top of the class on the morals front. They feel nothing so they can squeeze you dry without a wisp of remorse.

Envy

This is my weak area. Even if in terms of success, I'm cooking on gas, if I suddenly see someone with more, I get that kick in the stomach, that stab in my heart that means I want him dead. I am the first to step forward and admit, I want what the next guy has. No matter what it is, I want it. Sometimes I get the lust for things I don't even want. I'm so ashamed of this but in the throes of envy, if I accidentally pick up *Tatler*, *Hello* or *Harpers* and I see Lord and Lady Pomkelson Pompel Pomp sipping champers, with their smiling teeth yapping at some opening of something (I would shoot myself if I were actually there), I can't help feeling that old gutter-rat sense of envy bubbling below the surface. If you ever hear me say, 'I'm so happy you got that job I always wanted', believe me, I not only want you dead but your whole family wiped out. I used to tear out pages of *Hello* magazine going, 'Die, die, die'.

I'm always checking how many tweets other people have compared to me to make myself crazy. I look at Stephen Fry's Twitter when I'm feeling particularly suicidal. He always inspires me when I need my envy stoking up. It's like that spot on your gums that hurts when you stick a pin in it but you can't stop doing it.

If only humans had a cookbook to see what our ingredients are. We could look up 'envy' and see that we all have it; it comes with the human package. It's just one of those things that kept us alive when we roamed the ancient Savannah. It's part of the survival-of-the-fittest kit, so that if one *Homo erectus* had an attractive pointed stone, we all wanted it and so we made our own pointed stone or even better smashed in his skull with a stick and stole his. It is in our biology, this reptilian feeling of wanting what the next guy has. We can see it in the 'hubris' of Greek drama. In every one of those Grecian plots, if someone got too big for their boots, divine justice would drop by and make them poke out their own eyes or accidentally screw their mother and then take poison. And now, we throw parties for people who have been promoted; though some of us afflicted ones hope they choke.

Rage

Your emotionally underdeveloped area may be anger, a very common ailment in the human psyche. It's left over from when we were basic grunt, kill and mate apes. This is how it manifests itself now; you see yourself as a perfectly civilized person, law-abiding, popular with friends and a respected citizen. Then something in you flips and triggers some alien rage that turns you from Jekyll to Hyde in a second: could be a traffic warden, could be your secretary who forgot to give you a message, could be your husband/wife who got lost again because he/she can't read a roadmap. Suddenly you're unrecognizable: lips back, teeth bared, a terrifying vomiting bark emitting from your throat as you verbally bully your victim to dust. You want to hammer them but the fear of prison holds you back by a thread. Usually after the incident you get the backwash, the poison you shot out comes right back at you and you suffer the hangover of shame and guilt until they drain from your system or you ask God to forgive you.

Deception

Don't be too hard on yourself; we are born with this one too. If we want something, we have the inbuilt skill to manipulate the situation in our favour. We can gazump someone's chances of getting the job, partner, money, you name it. We have the ability to outfox. We know how to smile but underneath we are plotting to overthrow them; talking behind their back, pretending to be happy for them and then hacking their phones. We are still animals under the skin; shifty and devious for survival's sake. Evolution has even provided facial expressions to throw people off the trail so we can succeed with our deception.

Facial Expressions

Before we had words, we spread the news using our facial expressions and to this day no matter where you are on the planet, even if you're born blind, by ten months you'll know how to pull up both sides of your mouth and smile; a real one, not that thing airline stewardesses do when they give everyone 'bye bye bye bye bye' like they have a bad stutter. Nature in its brilliance made sure the first expression a baby learns is a smile because if it didn't smile we would have tossed that screaming glob of fat (who can't even go to the loo by itself) away. To this day people will tolerate and even love you if you smile. People in showbiz have this pummelled into them, singing to themselves, 'Smile though your heart is breaking, smile even though you're faking . . . smile and the world smiles with you.'

Whether you live in Bora Bora or Detroit, the facial expression for anger remains the same. It can be recognized by a drawing back of the lips and showing teeth, which demonstrates to others that you could eat them if pushed. The exposed teeth were to show how sharp they were. How white they were was irrelevant. The growling was dropped once we learnt to swear. We show disgust by flaring our nostrils and putting our mouths in an 'ick' shape to show others around us that, let's say, the fish is off. Fear is easy to spot: the open-mouthed screaming and bulging eyes gives a big clue for those nearby to run. Surprise is an intake of breath with an open mouth, warning others that something is not as it should be. It could be something bad or good; it's sort of the human version of a yellow light.

Laughter begins as a half scream from the shocked response of seeing something unexpected – a man slipping on a banana. You're about to express alarm but when you realize the danger has passed, that he's still alive, your lips draw up and your eyes crinkle to show others that there is no emergency. Humour comes from shock followed by relief, expressed by a barking noise. It indicates that this is a joke, not an actual catastrophe and the bark is so ludicrous, so infectious, that others around you also bark and clap their hands, all joining in the celebration that the pie in the face was not serious. Everyone is so relieved they bark some more.

We're born with the 47 facial muscles that create our expressions. All of our emotional states are viscerally connected to our facial muscles so we can read each other loud and clear, underneath language. Watch a silent movie and get back to me.

We developed facial expressions not just to read each other but also to deceive each other. For example, if you found food and you didn't want anyone to get it, you could fake a look of disgust then everyone leaves and you get the meat. Those who were best at deception survived and the suckers fell by the wayside. This remains the same today. This *schadenfreude* face is one of the ugliest of all expressions. It means, I'm-so-happy-sorry-but-mostly-I'm-happy-you've-been-demoted-or-even-better-fired. If you watch a face it will tell you everything. For instance you cannot fake a smile. There is a muscle under the eye called the periocular that will not become active if you aren't genuinely smiling. The mouth is easy to upturn but if you don't find something funny, that periocular muscle just doesn't move; your eyes are dead as a trout's.

Learning to read faces should be compulsory in schools so you can decipher what people are really thinking. Imagine if we could spot politicians right off the bat when they're lying, they'd all be out of work in a week. Someone should have walked out of Bernard Madoff's office and screamed, warning others (with his mouth wide open and fear in the eyes and then flared his nostrils to show disgust): 'This man is a maniac!' Then all those people wouldn't have lost $50 bn. If we were taught in school how to read faces, we could have spotted those sociopathic mortgage lenders and noticed they had the eyes of lizards.

Jealousy

I wish we could express this emotion like kids do. If someone gets something you want, you just hit them over the head and snatch it back. That's why children are so un-neurotic. They are doing what we only dream of.

The Road to Wisdom

First thing on the road to wisdom is to face ourselves honestly. People used to call it baring your soul, I call it looking in the mirror and cutting the bullshit. Here's how I read the situation. You may see it a totally different way but I'm the one writing this book so it's pretty much going to be my opinion.

Because of this faulty plumbing, we're anxious, angry, fearful, stressed and depressed and we try to put the blame on what's going on in the world. We blame it on climate change, the Muslims, the Jews, the banks and whoever happens to be president or prime minister. The names change, they come and go; we hate them all. We love them in the beginning, then turn on them and say, 'It's all their fault we're in a mess'. But I say to you, we put them in there, we voted for them. The problem lies in us, we are always in conflict, and so that is how we see the world. Inside our heads there is always war. Bob Geldof says, 'We are the world'. We are, he didn't mean it in a nasty way but I do. It's all our fault; no one else is in the driver's seat, just us.

Many people want to change the world; they don't want to change themselves.

Wisdom isn't something they ever write about in *Vogue* or can sell at Harvey Nichols. I wish it were, it would be so convenient while shopping for shoes. We used to have people we could ask these more existential questions. Where are they now? Out of work, like everyone else.

'Life is meaningless, God is dead.' Oh please, I'm depressed enough. Imagine if Sartre did stand up, the whole room would slash their wrists. Most of us don't have old Shaman grandmothers sitting on their haunches, breasts pointing to the floor, handing down their knowledge. My grandmother couldn't even tell me where she left her teeth, let alone any wisdom.

We spend a whole lifetime hunting for some wisdom. In childhood, it's 'happy days', our biggest challenge is hitting the potty, after that the shit hits the fan. By the time you hit your 20s you're fuelled with the stress that you have to end up as someone special. Clearly some give up and just take root on their sofas but most young folks feel they have to turn on the turbo and go for the gold. In your 30s you're fighting to keep what you've got and by your 50s you know it's going to get taken away. And this is where the road divides and you either turn into wine or into vinegar.

If you live long enough, a miracle might happen. If you make it to 83½, just when you look like a walking Lucian Freud painting, you might become wise. But it has to be that late in the day: you cannot be a babe and wise, it's against the laws of nature. But if you make it to 83½ and you don't get overwhelmed by fear that makes you withdraw into your past, boring everyone senseless, and if your mind stays flexible and curious and you ask people questions and listen to their answer, and if you let all your narcissism, resentment, regret and envy drain out of you and you finally realize that the world will be fine without you, then you're wise.

My Search for Normality

Perhaps I've come across as too negative in the book so far. I assume that what I'm writing about is our general malaise; what all people feel deep inside. I might be wrong, I've gotten things wrong before and I'll admit I'm not an expert on what 'normal' people feel if they indeed exist. So I apologize if you're sitting there going, 'What the hell is she on about? We don't think about any of these things. We live a happy and healthy life. Let's give this book to Uncle Psycho.'

I didn't mean to insult any of you. On the contrary, I am a great admirer of people who believe they are normal, I am fascinated by them. I've always thought, is it possible to feel the way Tony Robbins looks? Confident, positive, flowing with love for himself with his big wall-to-wall teeth and large genitalia. (I am guessing about this but he has a very large nose and I connect the two.) What makes him so sure he's right? Does he really believe the script that is pouring out of his mouth? Is that normal?

I obsessively eavesdrop in public places (bars, trains, buses, restaurants) with my ear almost in the fruit salad in my search for who might be normal. I listen in to a conversation in a bar where a seemingly normal group of good old boys, team-mates who work together, making valves for garbage disposals, are all out to celebrate the up-and-coming plumbing awards for which they have gathered. They seem so content with their lot; a happy pack at the watering hole, clinking glasses, toasting one another for the fact that they're up to win 'Plumbing Team of The Year', fantasizing their names are being called out, hitting the air with their fists as they hear in their heads the music playing, 'You're the Best', then each one of them makes a little slurry speech about how they couldn't have done it without their team, posing for an imaginary photo, giving each other slaps on the back. Is that normal?

I've listened in to a girl at the next table in a restaurant, panting with excitement as she asks her friend to be her maid of honour at her wedding and the friend bursting into tears and blibbing on about how she'll be the best maid of honour that ever lived and can't wait to help choose the napkin colour . . . Is that normal?

I sit in a hotel lobby and listen in to two cigars with fat men on the ends yabbing about the price of housing, throwing out percentages of the increase or decrease of the market with complete confidence about how right they are. How does anyone accurately know how much a house price is going to rise or fall and who cares? Is that normal?

Everyone's an Expert Except Me

At dinner parties, I hear people locked in debate about how to resolve the crisis in the Middle East like they're experts. 'Here's what I would tell the Taliban.' The president couldn't figure it out with his advisors but these 'if you ask me' people presume to know. They base their extensive knowledge on the same newspaper everyone else reads; yet they have the answer. Where does that confidence come from? Around the world everyone is an 'expert'. There must be at this very second 64 billion experts having coffee and giving their opinions on climate change, nuclear disarmament, obesity and the war on drugs.

I sat next to a man telling me what the Flemish were thinking during the Second World War. I was dripping in sweat thinking, 'Should I know that information? Will he think I'm an idiot when he finds out I know nothing about the topic and is there going to be a quiz?' I don't even know where Flemmark is. I have to sit there, dying inside with self-loathing, while the Flem expert whips out more information like a swinging dick.

This exhibiting of 'the one big dick' memorized fact is how we unconsciously determine who the alpha is at the dinner table. Lecturing on Flemland to people who have no idea is the same as the chief gorilla beating his chest to show who is boss. This Flem guy somehow senses that I know nothing and I'm sinking in a mound of self-hatred, so he feels triumphant – he's won that round until he meets a bigger expert on Flem matters.

People find their scrap of knowledge and unquestioningly live their lives gathering their little pile of research then boring people senseless with the details.

To be honest, the main reason I listen in is to find someone, someday that might come out with some Earth-shattering revelation and I will scream, 'Aha! Bingo! That is the answer to why we exist.' It hasn't happened yet but I'm always on the look-out. My suspicion is that we're all wondering what 'normal' feels like; all believing the next guy knows but not us. This may just be the way I think so forgive me if you don't agree. I do know that we all want to be happy and we spend a great deal of our lives hunting for the key. No matter how powerful or successful we get, we still can't figure out how to deal with a mind that keeps us up at night, driving us to exhaustion. This isn't just for those who are considered mad, it's for all of us. I wish we could just come out and say how we really feel; I know I'd be so relieved.

Part Two

What's Wrong With Us?
For the Mad-Mad

Depression - Broken Brains

I'm going to start with my own story as throughout my life I have had ever-increasing episodes of depression. I hope others can identify even if they don't have the full-blown illness. We are all, at times, at the mercy of our more compulsive and fearful emotions and have no means to find a way out.

My Story

It was World Mental Health Day and I was asked to go on the BBC World Service to talk about depression. I happened to be suffering very badly but didn't want to say so, even though I was talking about the need to end the stigma. I was wearing sunglasses during the interview and should have taken them off and said, 'Do you want to see what depression looks like? Here it is.' I was too ill to think that far out of the box, my only concern was getting through it without breaking down on air.

As soon as I finished the show, I asked the driver to take me to the Priory, to my doctor Mark Collins, to up the dosage of my medication. This had already happened a few years earlier when I had depression while filming a TV show and insisted on hiding it. The show was about various mental illnesses and each week we would film at my house. My doorbell would ring and there would be someone with either ADHD, schizophrenia, OCD, bipolar disorder, bulimia, physical dysmorphia, you name it, I had it over for tea. The problem was, during the first few shows I happened to be in the Priory and I didn't want anyone to know for fear of losing my job. My husband would pick me up; all the other inmates looked at me like I was crazy (high praise from the experts) as I was driven home to interview someone with a mental illness without saying a word about how sick I was. When it was over, my husband would drive me back, I'd get back into my pyjamas and go to bed.

I'm wary about harping on about depression. People glaze over; you can see them thinking, 'Oh here she goes again, jawing on about "the darkness".' Once you couldn't say 'gay' and before that it was the 'C' word and further back you couldn't even mention you were a witch – depression is the latest taboo.

And this isn't something that happens to a small minority, it's up to one in four of us, so where is everyone? If it's not you it's probably a relative or a friend – everyone knows someone. When Hamlet says, 'O, that this too too solid flesh would melt, thaw and resolve itself into a dew!' That's got to be one of the most accurate descriptions of depression. (If a shrink heard you say that he'd have you on meds in seconds.) Part of the stigma lies in the fact that the word 'depressed' depicts a kind of 'down in the dumps' sentiment. Sadness or unhappiness is perfectly normal if something has not turned out the way you wanted it to or someone has died.

Depression is a whole other beast; it is not situation

appropriate. Here's something you get absolutely free with this illness: a real sense of shame; it comes with the package. And you feel such extreme shame because you think, 'I'm not being carpet-bombed, I don't live in a township.' Your thoughts become so punishing for your selfishness – like bombs, incoming over Dresden – so loud, so relentless you get not one voice but about 100,000 abusive voices; like if the Devil had Tourette's. Depression doesn't care if you're famous, live in a mud hut or what culture you come from, it just loves everyone.

Those of you who do suffer know that we just need to look in each other's eyes and we recognize that we have the 'illness'. It's like a secret handshake. You can read depression loud and clear if you look into the eyes of a sufferer; there's no mistaking it, it's the look of a dead shark. Most people don't really look closely so they'd miss this detail. Teachers should be trained to notice that look in their students to get them help before the 'cutting' starts or worse, a suicide.

My Story

Here's a coincidence. I'm having a bout of depression right now as I'm writing this book. So I'm going to just write down my experience as it happens. If it was an acute episode I wouldn't be able to type these words; I wouldn't be able to connect one thought with the next or even comprehend the meaning of words; I would bury this computer in a closet, sit on a chair and wait to be institutionalized.

Luckily, due to practising mindfulness, I have an early warning system. It can't eliminate depression but I can hear the alarms before it eats me alive. This is why I can continue to write. I'm aware I'm just in the foothills of depression, but I can hear the far-off footsteps of the negative, derogatory thoughts like a Zulu tribe creeping up on me.

There are clues that something is wrong because I can only sleep two hours at a time and when I wake there is dread; heavy like a weight on my chest. My movement is limited and trips to the shower are like getting ready for a decathlon. I have to pep talk myself up with, 'Come on Ruby, you can do it, one step at a time. It's just your illness, it's not you. You will come back, it's just an illness.' And then of course I'm aware of the infamous to-do list, which starts like that giant round boulder chasing Harrison Ford in *Raiders of the Lost Ark*. I try to figure out why I feel the cannonball compulsion to go out and purchase things on the list. I try to question the thinking that tells me, 'If I could only get through that list, I'd be fine.'

Another mental torture arises from the fact that I'm being haunted continuously by the thought of how old I am and how many years I have left. I have been doing this periodically since I was 40; now I do it all the time. Each day I look for signs of my decay and, in finding them, feel my own imminent death.

I'm also becoming obsessed that I need to buy blue-and-white-striped cushion covers. (The shame, the shame.) I have spent six hours on my computer scanning for nautical covers and I hunted some down in

Canada and some in Mexico; it took me four more hours to figure out how to use the credit card, I was shaking so much. Some have actually been sent to me and they are too tiny, much tinier than in the photo on the website and cost £93. I want to send them back but am paralyzed by the certainty that I don't know how to do that. Now I am consumed with self-loathing; I spent all that time choosing them and now they look like bits of tissue paper with stripes; cheap, awful. I am left with a picture in my head of my ideal striped cushions, fixating about where I can locate them.

I already had this obsession recently about lamps. I had arrived in London and I actually made my taxi driver stop on the way back from the airport as I leapt across busy traffic, nearly being hit by a truck on my way to a lamp shop. It didn't have exactly what I was picturing so I leapt out another six times. I told the driver it was an emergency (what emergency could be happening in Habitat?) I finally bought a round plastic garden lamp, which is all wrong. It changes colour and looks hideous. So I'm still on the look-out for a lamp but now I also need those cushion covers. I had been in Ireland doing a job, which was why I was coming home from the airport, and I hadn't seen my children for a long time. What am I doing? I'm jumping from shop to shop to find lamps. Wouldn't you hate yourself if this were you?

The feeling is that of being a corpse, no sense of skin or other extremities, like fingers or legs. I'm this empty thing now and honestly have no recollection of the chutzpah I had only last week. Now nothing is anything, and everything is nothingness, just the cannons of pressure going off in my head. It's as if your old personality has been sucked out so slowly that you didn't notice its departure. Very slowly it's been stolen away and each day you remember less and less of who you are and what you feel.

I want to try and go to John Lewis but I know I will get there and wander like a nomad, lost and unable to remember why I went. This is why people think depression is something you make up; how could I convince someone that my thoughts are bombarding me with household goods? This could be why there's a stigma – anyone in their right mind would say, 'What the hell is wrong with you? Why would we give money for researching a cure when the problem is getting a cushion? Am I supposed to take that seriously?' They'd say, 'Come on, people are dying of cancer. They wouldn't know a cushion if it came up and spoke to them.' I want to tell them that the *voice* telling me to get the cushion is the illness. People don't commit suicide because they can't find a cushion but the feeling of helplessness, the sense that your brain does not belong to you anymore with its insane commands, could drive you over a cliff just to get some quiet.

As I say, I am only in the foothills and simply noticing what my thoughts are gives me whole seconds where I know that those thoughts are the illness; they are not me. So I am in the depression, knee-deep, not over my head yet. I'll keep you posted, though you might know anyway because this book may never get written.

NEXT DAY STILL DEPRESSED

I'm writing again the next day and yesterday after the unsuccessful hunt of the lamp and cushions, my girlfriend Kathy Lette asked me to come over for dinner along with (I kid you not) Gordon and Sarah Brown, Neil and Glenys Kinnock and Jemima Khan. I am so crazy that while Kathy's asking me over, I am on the internet looking at a cushion.

In the old days, at this point in my depression, I would have run upstairs to get dressed thinking I needed to meet these people for some reason. I would have brushed aside the fact I was ill, jumped in my car and driven, wild at the wheel, sweating, probably getting seriously lost and crashing several times before finally arriving and trying to look nonchalant. Then I'd drink too much to overcome my fear that they'd see I'm an idiot and suss that I know nothing. They would be talking about the Labour Party while I would be internally vomiting trying to add something enlightening to these leaders of Labour. The evening would end with me drunk, nearly in passing-out state, trying to be funny, taking over the room and slurring about how much I loved my dead dog. Somehow I would find myself at home without knowing how I got there and think about suicide.

NEXT DAY

So another day passes and I get up exhausted remembering that my TED Talk goes live on air today and I'm at level ten of anxious; assuming that no one will watch it and those who do will think TED is now getting idiots on. I'm feeling like I'm walking towards the lions in the Colosseum because I know that however great I should feel about being on TED there will inevitably be that wrenching agony just around the corner that they will pull it off the air because I get a unanimous thumbs down from the viewers. I know that whenever something good happens or I've actually accomplished something and feel a glimmer of pride I am pretty much immediately kicked in the ass by karma. Also, today, most importantly, I decide I have to have a white carpet to match the cushions. I had one, which is now missing and I am screaming at everyone in my house because I am convinced someone stole it. 'Where is it? Who took it?'

I am now Googling carpets, ignoring my children who want to tell me something but I have to find the perfect one and when I see one I like, I use that tiny magnifying glass on the photo that lets you see the pile up-close with a hand stroking it (just a hand, no body) up and down, as if you could feel it yourself. I'm judging how it feels and then move on to another site to imagine feeling other rugs.

At this moment my only relief is the image of the blue-and-white-striped cushions, when I think of the blue I feel calmer, otherwise I cannot see colours, the world inside is black-and-white. I wish it was an image of something inspired or sacred rather than a cushion but I'm only telling you this so you get an idea of the obsessive, mind-numbing weight of this disease.

Fingers crossed I will find the cushion, the lamp and the carpet.

Facts About Depression

- The current annual economic cost of mental illness in the UK is £70 billion, which is equal to the entire National Health budget .

- By 2030, the World Health Organization predicts more people will be affected by depression than any other health problem.

- It already affects more people than all physical illnesses put together.

- Mental illness accounts for nearly half of all people on incapacity benefits in the UK. The official figure is 44%.

- The World Economic Forum estimates that the global cost of mental illness will be about $16 trillion by 2030. Uni-polar depressive disorders are the third biggest global burden in the world.

- Mental illness affects people early (50% of cases occur by age 14).

- Mental health problems also increase the risk of physical illness. People with schizophrenia and bipolar disorder die on average 16-25 years sooner than the general population.

- Data accrued from six European countries found that 17% of the population reported some experience with depression in the last six months.

- At any one time, 10% of the US population has experienced clinical depression in the past year and between 20-25% women and 7-12% men will suffer a clinical depression during their lifetimes.

What Do We Do About Depression?

So here's the million-dollar question: what do we do about mental illness? If therapy and drugs are working why is it on the increase? And how does a GP know how to make a correct diagnosis in ten minutes? Each one of us is different. And we are so complicated, how would they find the right cocktail for you? It's a zillion to one crap shoot especially as the drugs themselves are archaic (taking an anti-depressant is like burning down the whole forest because one tree is diseased) but at the moment they are all we have.

Fellow sufferers have asked me how to deal with their illness. Here it is. This is what I would say to anyone who has a mental illness themselves or has a family member, friend or co-worker who is suffering: tell them to find someone else who has what they have, whatever the illness. They are not hard to locate: they are one in four of the population, remember? You don't need to be Sherlock Holmes.

Half of the cure is realizing that you are not alone, that this 'illness' actually exists like any other physical illness; you are not making it up and you are not some self-indulgent, self-obsessed narcissist who's looking for pity or an excuse not show up at work or school. Find someone who shares your pain. Go and locate what I call a 'fucked buddy' – someone you can always call, day or night, when you can't take it anymore.

If you talk to people who don't understand they will nod and say how sorry they are and tell you to try and get better but they cannot feel it and will eventually get bored or, in extreme cases, leave you. (So many people have told me that they've been abandoned when they were in the depths of depression.) If you find someone who has what you have, they will never get bored; they will talk drugs, voices and heartache with you till the cows come home. They will relate and resonate with you, holding your hand through the agony.

My Suggestions (A Diatribe)

Alcoholics Anonymous has a system where you call your 'buddy' when you feel you want a drink and they will talk you down. Why can't we have meeting places like in AA, where they all get together for their 12-step thing and have cigarettes and cookies? How did they organize these get-togethers so well? They have meeting places on every corner of every block; more places than there are Starbucks and these people are drunks? How did they figure all this out? Why can't we do that? We're just as discriminated against as alcoholics; if you ever write that you suffer from a mental disorder on your CV, good luck ever landing a job. If you run a company and you've taken off more than six months because of a mental problem, you're fired. It should be against the law, just as it is with someone physically disabled.

The gays turned it around in my lifetime, now they're every-where: politicians, CEOs, generals, lords, hairdressers . . . Let's go find where they keep their old rainbow banners, high-heels and tutus that they wore during their gay parades, put them on and march to parliament with pitch forks screaming, 'WE ARE MENTALLY ILL, WE ARE THE ONE IN FOUR AND PROUD. CHANGE THE LAWS. WE ARE LIKE EVERYONE ELSE.' Maybe if we do this we won't have to hunker down in isolation any more, quivering in case someone we know finds out, or worse someone at work finds out and we're either dismissed (the company probably will say for other reasons) or treated like a person with Ebola. Ok, that's my suggestion. Take it or leave it. My political rant is over.

Reality of Mental Illness – In the Brain

Depression is the result of something going wrong somewhere in the brain. We only perceive the world outside because of our brain: everything you dream or create, what you laugh or cry about, hope for or imagine, who you worship or love, whenever you dance Zumba, pole vault, make pumpkin pie, hold up a bank, it is all because of some activity in the brain.

I'll give you a few examples of some of the physical ramifications that affect your behaviour if you get whacked in any specific region of the brain or you suffer from a tumour.

If, for example, you damage an area in the temporal lobe it may result in a syndrome known as prosopagnosia or face blindness. This means you will no longer be able to recognize people's faces. So your mother may be standing in front of you and you will have no clue who this woman is, even though you can see her clearly. (I wish I had that problem.)

Capgras syndrome is also caused by damage in the fusiform gyrus but in this case you are under the illusion that your mother is an imposter. You would say this person looks like your mother but it is not her, it is someone identical. This is thought to happen if brain pathways that connect the face-processing areas to the limbic system (amygdala) have been severed or damaged. If your mother called you on the phone you would recognize her voice but if she was standing in front of you, you would not believe it was her.

Another example of cross-wiring in the brain producing abnormal behaviour is known as synesthesia. This can be genetically transmitted with the result that your senses are tangled. If for example, someone plays a D note on a piano, it might be perceived as yellow, or E is experienced as maroon. Others can see numbers as colours. They say Einstein had this; it must have been a psychedelic light-show in his brain. Again this is not a result of imagination, but because of damage or genetic factors.

Another syndrome known as pain asymbolia, also due to mis-wiring, has the result that a person responds to pain with uncontrollable laughter. Another person with pica disorder will eat things that are not edible; rocks, buttons, toys, doors, watches, blue-and-white-striped cushions (God forbid).

Damage to the right hemisphere of the brain may affect the left side of the body (the right brain controls the left side of the body and vice versa). If you have brain damage on the right side, you will not attend to what is being held up in front of you on your left side. Both eyes would be fine – it's just that your brain would not process any information in the left visual field. In really bad cases you'll ignore the left side of the world. You will only eat food off your plate on the right hand side and leave the food on the left. If you are a woman you will only put lipstick on the right side of your mouth. (This can be incredibly funny but it's best not to laugh at people with this syndrome. If you do, do it on the left side because you won't be seen.)

Then we have the very bizarre somatoparaphrenia. This is when you're unhappy with a certain part of your body so you ask to have it removed, i.e. an arm or leg, usually not your head. You have the delusion that this limb or side of your body does not belong to you. You are aware of it – it just doesn't seem to be part of you. This one requires a real hard bump on the head, stroke or epilepsy in the right hemisphere, especially the right temporoparietal junction, which is also the region responsible for so-called out-of-body experiences. So the experience that you are floating above your body, watching it from the outside, can be repeatedly evoked by stimulating this part of the brain in a laboratory. How many tickets to India could have been thrown out the window if people knew they could get this buzz in a lab?

Here's my personal favourite disorder: Cotard's syndrome. The sufferer claims he or she is dead. If you look at their brain in a scanner, you can see where the damage is that causes these thoughts. All senses become disconnected from the emotional centres in the brain; nothing has any emotional resonance so there is a complete cut-off from any reality. And so the person will assume they are dead. If you prick them with a pin and they bleed they will be surprised and conclude that the dead also bleed. A hundred years ago, the sufferer would have been called crazy or before that, burnt at the stake.

Here's my point, if Cotard's syndrome is considered a neurological malfunction that causes the sufferer to feel dead, why is depression, which shares the same circuitry and symptoms, not taken seriously. Duh? It's a no-brainer.

Vilayanur Ramachandran (to me, one of the most impressive of contemporary brain scientists) has done extensive research on these disorders and found that schizophrenia could also be described physiologically. Based on work he's done on anosognosia, caused by right-hemisphere lesions or damage, he has discovered that the sufferer becomes unaware that they are ill or impaired. They may be blind or paralyzed and believe that they are perfectly fine as they walk into walls. What's interesting is that anosognosics share the same symptoms with schizophrenics who cannot distinguish between what they think or imagine and what is really happening in the outside world, so that if they were imagining they were Marie Antoinette and were unaware of external reality, they might actually believe they were her. When schizophrenics move their bodies they often can't tell if they are moving it themselves or it is being moved by someone outside of themselves; which means they might come to the conclusion that perhaps aliens or Jennifer Aniston were in charge.

Brain-imaging research, PET scans, EEGs and fMRI (functional Magnetic Resonance Imaging) can explain why one guy is normal in every other way except that when he sees his uncle he sees a giraffe. Now you can just scan him and have a look. There it is, the reason for the odd behaviour or hallucination, clear as the nose on your face.

The brain (the actual organ) and the mind (moods, emotions, thoughts, memories, personality traits and all the information carried by your neurons) are intrinsically intertwined; they are co-dependent. If the brain is damaged so is the mind and alterations in brain chemistry cause changes in moods, memory and attention. So why is there such a stigma when it comes to mental illness when we know it is caused by genetics, disease, trauma or physical accidents?

My Story

About five years ago, I wrote a comedy/tragedy called *Losing It* with my friend Judith Owen (she wrote the music, I wrote the script). I had recently become the poster girl for mental illness, though in the past I wouldn't have mentioned I had depression, let alone written a show about it. The reason I was able to be open about my illness was because I was unintentionally 'outed' when Comic Relief asked me to pose for a photo to raise money for the mental health arm of their charity. I assumed it was going to be a discreet small stamp-sized photo in the back of some magazine.

Imagine my horror when I walked into a tube station and saw a gigantic poster of me with, 'This woman has mental illness can you help her?' written underneath. I was mortified and hurled myself onto the poster to hide it but there were too many so I kept hurling to no avail. I suddenly had a flash-bulb moment, I decided to write a show and pretend the poster was for my publicity. I thought, 'Ruby, if you've got a disability, use it.' I wrote the show and toured mental institutions for two years and if you can make a schizophrenic laugh, believe me, you're half-way to Broadway.

The show was performed at over 50 mental institutions around the UK; the Duchess Theatre, London; the Menier Chocolate Factory, London; and the Purple Cow at the Edinburgh Festival. At this point it evolved into my one-woman show, *Out of*

Her Mind, and played at the Broad Stage, Los Angeles, the Theatre on the Bay, Cape Town, South Africa and the Forum Theatre, Melbourne, Australia.

I still perform the show but my interest has dramatically shifted. I decided I would look into the actual brains, which make us how we are, because it really is the most interesting thing in the universe. Much more than the stars up there – they can look after themselves or Brian Cox can take care of them. Who is 'us'? That is the mystery. As I had just mentally imploded, this was probably the perfect time to address it.

BACK TO SCHOOL

So I thought, I'm 87 (not really), why not go back to school but this time listen and not get expelled for putting sardines under the lighting fixtures? Ok, I'll start over again. So I enrolled at Regent's College of Psychotherapy. On day one, I loved my new friends. I'd carry books like I used to in high school, piled high in my arms, and we'd all go to the cafeteria and get in a queue for awful hard lasagne and neon-pink dessert on a tray. I loved that. And no one treated me like I was even interesting. If you don't think of yourself as special no one else does either. People only notice you when you want to be noticed. Watch a famous person: they almost shine a spotlight in their own faces even though they pretend to want to be ignored. At the end of the day, we'd do group therapy and some of the more dominant girls and I formed a clique and we'd gang up on the weaker men. We'd roll our eyes and grunt whenever they spoke. Our circle got tighter as we defended each other saying we were strong not aggressive, working as a unit of bulldozers.

Weird things still happened as they did in my past. There were about 16 people on my course and they were a diverse bunch. One of my classmates had been a hooker in the past (I loved her). Now she wanted to help people rather than screw them. What a gal. It turns out she recognized one of our fellow students (a guy we hated as he was smug and sanctimonious) as being one of her ex-clients. Of all the people in the world he had to walk into that place and then into this class. The ex-hooker told me this in confidence; I guess she felt she could trust me to keep quiet. I kept my mouth shut for three years and, my God, was that hard when he belittled women. I never said a word and I still haven't: I'm writing it down.

But I loved my course. Each week we studied another great therapist and I believed each one and then the next week disbelieved him and went on to my next shrink crush.

Freud

Brilliant with the unconscious and what a concept that underneath your lid is the id, the furnace of hell that lies beneath all our frilly fronts. It is the ego that keeps up appearances, it's sort of our psychic underwear so we don't have to face the world exposed as the pathetic mess we really are. (I once had a Freudian analyst with whom I argued

about a cigar being just a cigar. He wouldn't have it
and told me I only said that because my father
made sausage casings and that was why I was so
screwed up. He kept trying to make me delve into
the fact I have a recurring dream that I'm sitting in
a box in the desert, covered in blood and faeces.
'It's no big deal, everyone has that dream,' I told
him. Also I told him about the dream I have where I
am on a plane and the tail breaks off and we have
to land in a narrow alley with the wing tips making
sparks on the brick walls, ending up in a quaint ski
resort in Switzerland. What's to figure out? I settled
my bill of £5000 an hour and walked out showing
him who was boss.)

Melanie Klein

She believed that Mommy had a good and a bad
breast and that could influence the mental condition
of an individual. I obviously got the wrong breast, the
evil one. (I forget if it's the right or left one.)

Jung

I loved him and the idea we have a shadow, a dark side,
and was so happy to find out it was a real address.

Carl Rogers

I also loved personal-centred therapy. Rogers just
reflected whatever you said back to you like a parrot
but with love. You would say something and then he'd
say, 'Do you mean?' followed by exactly what you said
back to you. Simple.

Gestalt

The acid trip of therapy. You get screamed at about what a fake and loser you are and somehow this helps you find the apple core of you, if you haven't had a nervous breakdown in the process. Not dissimilar to primal scream therapy where you relive your birth again but this time you've got a handgun.

Then came the existentialists, each more upsetting then the next:

Heidegger

What a guy. He wrote total gibberish putting dashes between-every-word-you-read.

Buber

If you address someone as 'thou' it means you really like them and acknowledge them as a fellow human. If you think of another person as 'an it' it means you are just using them to get what you want; they are a means to an end. He cleared up so much for me as far as sorting out the 'thous' from the 'its'.

Nietzsche

Impossible to spell; another colourful guy who said, 'God is dead' and we shouldn't raise our hopes.

Winnicott

I also loved him. He talked about the 'good enough' mother so I felt that he excused me for almost killing my children when I accidentally fed them rat pellets.

He said that as long as the mother meant well, the kid won't be screwed up. Thank you, Winnicott.

And finally Bowlby

Gave me all I needed to know as to why I was and am mentally ill. He divided care-giver/baby relationships into three types of attachment categories which exemplified your relationship to the world and to yourself. There's secure attachment when Mommy and Baby are in tune, googling away at each other. When Mommy leaves the room, Baby cries and wants her back and when she returns he goes to her for soothing. Ambivalent attachment is when Mommy leaves the room and Baby just sits there looking bored and then when she comes in looks even more bored and plays with some blocks. And then there is disorganized attachment; when Mommy leaves the room, Baby looks relieved and when she comes back, it screams. Guess which one I was?

To attain full qualification as a therapist, you have to work for 400 hours as an intern. I got to 200 and people were still asking me if my clients laughed when I came in the room to be their therapist. Actually, when I got my first client I was more nervous than I've ever been; I thought, what if they scream, 'You're a phony. I don't like you, get me someone else.' My concern wasn't that they would recognize me, it was the same fear that anyone new to the job would have: 'What the hell do I say to this person?'

Actually they didn't recognize me or care who I

was. They had bigger problems. A few of my clients were women who were held as slaves by their husband's families and threatened with death if they told anyone. I sat there and thought what an 'up-my-own-ass spoilt brat' I was to have ever thought I had problems. These mother-in-laws who splashed boiling water on their daughter-in-laws to show who was boss made my mother seem like Tinker Bell.

And the ones that were English, even if they recognized me, couldn't care less because they could feel that we had a lot in common. They'd talk about their loneliness and hopelessness and I really listened with compassion, which is the main point of shrinkdom. I felt it was an honour that they let me into their lives and I still wonder if I helped fix them, at least a little? I learnt that we're all such delicate creatures and many of us are in pain and it takes such bravery to just go on living.

I realized after working 200 hours that I was starting to lose compassion and I could never fake it. I think you either have to be insane or an angel to sit there and hold all that incoming pain. As it happened, perhaps just to test me, I was offered a bite at show business again while I was still working with abused women. What did I do? I grabbed at it like a heroin addict finding a needle. I still shudder at the memory and shame of what I did. You would have thought I had learnt my lesson from the *Shark Attack* incident, but no. I was asked to do a big prime-time game show, where I would be the master of ceremonies in a circus tent while F-list celebrities performed trapeze work with no net. A panel with some screaming queens would judge who was the bravest in this gladiatorial bloodbath.

I thought everyone concerned would know how grotesque this all was and I could poke fun at the desperate celebrities hanging by their toes to make a comeback or, in some cases, risking their lives to emerge from the cocoon of mediocrity as fully-winged TV personalities. Sadly this was not to be. They dressed me in a corset, gave me a whip and sent me into the ring. I was told to take it seriously and not to make fun of anyone, to keep my irony to myself. I was left without a comedy life raft as I had to say how magical the starlet was while she was hanging above me by her cervix, wearing a feather. I wanted to say how amazing it was that she had just come out of rehab but they made me shut up and say, 'Let's hear it for her, ladies and gentlemen. Give a round of applause to this remarkable woman.'

I read the autocue with tears pouring down my face while cranked in a hideous smile, eyes dead. Anyway they fired me, which was a lucky thing because I was still working as a therapist. At supervision sessions, where we went each week to get feedback on our work, the supervisor said maybe it wasn't a good idea for me to be a therapist at this time. I asked why?

She pointed out that I was on billboards throughout London half the size of a football field wearing my corset with my breasts in 3D hanging out of the picture and holding my whip; that perhaps some of my clients might think it strange. Perhaps she had a point.

So I thought, let's leave psychotherapy to the psychos and get into the meat; I'll learn how the brain works. I crashed a neuroscience course at UCL filled with 21-year-olds. I felt like a freak so I told them I had a skin disease; that one where you age really fast? Then they let me go out with them until they realized I really was old. Eventually the fetus-like students included me at lunchtime, mostly because I was the only one who drove and I could take them to the park.

The only science I had done was at high school when I once dissected a frog and put it in my friend's handbag, so I didn't come with a lot of credentials. There I was every week with my note-book, scribbling down how some sodium molecules pass through the synaptic wall by an electrical current thereby transporting neurotransmitters to the next neuron which happens over a trillion times in less than one-thousandth of a second. I didn't know what they were talking about but I took hundreds of pages of notes, all incomprehensible scribbles now. I could publish the notebooks and call it *The Art of a Madman*. In the end the rest of the class went on to Yale University to complete their masters. I remember them all waving me farewell because a) I was only crashing the course and b) I knew very little.

What's Wrong With Us? For the Mad-Mad

I thought, I've got to trump them going to Yale, so I did the only thing I could think of, I got into Oxford.

In years to come, anyone consulting the class of 2012 photograph from Oxford University's Kellogg College will see among the dignified students looking earnestly into the camera, a very mature (in attitude not years) student looking demented with happiness – that would be me.

My children are furious because I left and went to university before they did – let them find out what the empty nest feels like. I heard one say, 'Our mother's left home. She's at freshers' week and we can't find her.' Before even the first class began, I had to do something called matriculation. I had no idea what that word meant, it sounded like an infection, but the next thing I knew, I was in full bat cape and square hat walking with hundreds of other students down Oxford High Street with common people cheering. I waved like the queen. As a student who never got the hang of spelling, you can imagine how startling the experience was.

You file into some ancient building and then the Dean of Deans dressed like a grand magician, welcomes you by saying, in Latin, 'Welcome! Now you are in the most holy of holy institutions.' At that point, I could only think that if I could dig up my parents and they could see this, they would never believe what was going on. Their heads wouldn't just spin as the saying goes, they would fall off.

It was very strange to me that I suddenly started

reading science books so voraciously at this time in my life. It was as if my old self had died and been taken over by a nerd. When did I turn into this? It seems I had reinvented my new self into a groupie for neuroscience; a fanatic follower. So after two years at Oxford University, here is my spin on Neuroscience.

Part Three

What's in Your Brain/
What's on Your Mind?

Why Neuroscience?

In order to get to know who you are and how you work, you need to metaphorically open the bonnet and look in at the engine. Freud, who originally wanted to be a neurologist, had to guess what was going on inside because in those days the only way you could study the brain was by hanging around a corpse. A dead brain is not ticking so it doesn't help. Now we can look in and see how neurons connect to different areas of the brain and watch the electrical and chemical power working throughout to create our thoughts, dreams, hopes, memories, emotions – everything.

We are the result of those connections, those chemical exchanges and of regions communicating with other regions. Some people believe this thinking is too reductionist and say disapprovingly, 'Is that all we are?' I feel we should be saying, 'Oh my God, I am all this?' Because what we are is so complex and extraordinary; how your brain works makes every other invention and accomplishment look like learning to fold a napkin.

For me, this has been the greatest 'aha' moment to end all 'aha's in my life so far. When you begin to grasp how every part of your brain has a function (valuing, thinking, moving, feeling), when you realize it's the subtle (and not so subtle) differences in our brain biology that make you you and me me, you'll also go, 'Aha'. Then you'll think, 'We absolutely must have the instruction manual for this thing' and you might even start stalking neuroscientists like I did.

As far as reality checks go, it can't get better than having a look at the real thing. Each one of our brains looks fairly similar when you crack us open, which to me is so comforting; to know I'm not alone and that we are all brothers under the skin. No light versus dark souls; just a dull pink. The best news of all is that we have reached a point in our development as a species where we can choose how our brains will react to events so that we're not held entirely captive by our old habits and biases, programming and mental blind spots. Most people don't know that this self-regulatory part comes with the package. We're born with this ability but sadly this information isn't imparted to the public (perhaps it wouldn't sell as many books as *75 Shades of Grey*).

When you learn how to use your mind as it can be used, you might even feel that elusive thing called 'happiness' or 'peace'. Yet what is known so far in terms of brain science doesn't seem to trickle down to the masses nor does the public seem to want it to trickle. Scientific information about the brain is based on hard evidence from a number of sources, including most recently advances in neuroimaging. These provide vivid pictures of the brain's components and associated functions. Neuroscience as a subject is still on the nursery slopes for the most part, as it is extremely complicated, but they've already learnt a huge amount about functions of our brains and the different areas involved when we add numbers, speak, make decisions, remember, hear, see and stay busy. If you doubt the empirical evidence but you do believe you've seen a UFO, please put this book down. It is not for you.

By watching how our thoughts affect the structure of the brain we're learning new ways we can consciously re-shape our own brains. Self-regulation means we can actually rewire our own brains by moving activity from one region to another, switching on diverse hormones that can stimulate us or calm us down.

In my opinion, learning this ability to self-regulate is the post-therapy zeitgeist. Evidence of how the brain changes can be seen in brain-imaging scanners and the results are published in scientific journals. Why isn't this the hottest news in town? You meet people who insist they know how the world works and themselves by how they feel. It's like insisting that the world is flat because they feel it is. I know change is painful to us all; old ways are always being replaced by the new. Soothsayers suddenly found themselves out of a job and alchemists were made redundant because people stopped needing their pigs turned into gold, or whatever it was they did. Some day we will laugh our heads off when we remember that a doctor didn't look inside your brain before he wrote you out a prescription. I'm not saying that by simply looking at an image in a scanner we'll know everything there is to know because it is true that who we are is also the result of our interactions with our parents, our environment, our learning and our culture. So in order to get to the bottom of the 21st-century problems we find ourselves facing, we'll need not only to learn about the basic functional architecture of the human brain but our personal story and our evolutionary story.

Here, based on scientific evidence, neuroscience and evolution are some answers to the questions raised in Part 1. Enjoy.

The Answer to 'Why the Critical Voices?'

We have this proclivity for negative nagging voices in our head because of that old fly in the works, survival. Every cell in us wants us to last long enough to pass the genes then we can go to hell as far as they're concerned. Part of our brain still thinks it's 400 million years ago so that we're on the constant look-out for predators who once killed us. Even in a resting state your brain is still tracking the horizon because back then there was so much lurking and we could do something about it, like run. Now, it's not enough to just run from what we perceive as threatening; we're helpless in the face of 21st-century danger: economic bedlam, out-of-control climate and crazy countries that might be hiding bombs. No wonder we're stressed.

This is why we're over-vigilant with paranoid feedback: 'Look out for that . . . don't screw up . . . those people hate you'. You're reacting just like your cat that hunches his back and hisses but you're hunching with words. It's the anxiety that keeps you on your toes. Close your eyes for a second, take your eye off the button and you're lunch. You can see why a glass half empty is our natural state.

The brain detects negative information faster than it does positive. We are drawn to bad news. When something is flagged as a negative experience, the hippocampus (responsible for consolidating memory) makes sure it's stored in an easy–to–reach place for future reference. If you whistled a happy tune and just thought lovely thoughts you'd probably be hit by a truck pretty quickly, and find yourself as road kill. This negative bias primes you for avoidance and fear but when you direct it at yourself, it can bring you to your knees with depression.

The Answer to 'Why We Never Have Enough?'

Science tells us that the reason we 'want' is that we are driven by a chemical in our brains called dopamine and when we get something we want, we reward ourselves with a hit of it, which creates a buzz, a kick, a thrill. It's like cocaine (which I never tried but heard about from other people, I won't name names, but I was told it is the same high). If you lust after something very badly (say a pair of shoes) and then manage to buy them, you get a dollop of dopamine, which motivates you to immediately start planning how to get the next pair. (This insane version of forward-planning was handed down from when we foraged for nuts or whatever we foraged for hundreds of millions of years ago. We'd find nuts, eat them and then immediately start making mental roadmaps of where to find other nuts in a similar terrain to the one we just scored in. We probably didn't even notice we were eating the nuts we were so busy thinking about our next forage.)

But back to shoes. These days with the ants in your pants from the dopamine, you'll need to find out how and where to get more shoes so you'll begin to close in on shoe-rich environments, i.e. malls. You'll start sniffing around Jimmy Choo shops and might even empty your bank account to buy some and the more you make that connection between malls and buying Jimmy Choos the more entrenched and deeper that habit gets. After a while even if you just smell a Jimmy Choo shoe, your dopamine will run riot. If you go to a fancy dinner party and someone is wearing a Jimmy Choo shoe, you're now so primed up to 'get shoe' that you might gnaw her foot off to get that buzz of excitement back again. With dopamine it's the craving; that's the thing that drives you, not the actual shoe. It's the chase – the thrill of the hunt driven on by cues in the environment that predict the next shoe around the corner. Dopamine does not always generate pleasure but impels you to seek rewards. You can be a very unhappy addict.

If, on the other hand, you don't get the shoes, the dopamine decreases in your system so you start to get feelings of withdrawal similar to having cold turkey from a drug; you get all itchy and scratchy like Billie Holiday was in the film. You're informed about this by a part of your brain called the basal ganglia, which acts as a thermostat, registering stimulation coming in from the senses. Once the hunt becomes less novel you lose that motivational 'oomph'.

At first, the basal ganglia is your best friend, it gets you high, you're cooking on gas, you 'wanna' party but when you can't get enough, *boom*, you're a junkie on skid row. We are our own walking pharmacies shooting ourselves up with our own homemade chemicals. This constant need for a fix to make you feel good prompts you to pursue rewards over and over again and strengthens the behaviour that made you want to get them in the first place. It's a vicious circle.

So the reward system is necessary for your survival; you can use it for positive effect in order to increase your motivation for the healthy feeling of satisfaction for a job well done. But it can also push you so much into over-drive it will run you ragged in your desire to achieve the unachievable. We need to be aware of each of our individual *tipping points* to differentiate between when we are on a high of creativity and production and when we are burning the engine. Our culture promotes an endless need for fulfillment to always want what the next guy has, even though the effort might kill us.

A Little History of How They Found Out 'What's Where' in the Brain

Having answered some of the questions raised in Part 1, I am going to name names as far as the mechanisms of the brain go, so that when I discuss mindfulness in Part 4 you'll see how you can intentionally change the physiology of your brain (neuroplasticity) and therefore regulate your thoughts and feelings.

In 1861, the French anatomist Pierre-Paul Broca opened the brain of a patient (after he was dead) who could only speak the single syllable 'tan'. That's all. Imagine going on a date with this guy – repetitive or what? Anyway, Dr Broca noticed a lesion growing toward the back of the frontal lobes and came up with the idea that it was this damage that was the cause of the speech problem. Broca decided that this must be the area responsible for speech and called it Broca's area. Tan couldn't argue. All he could say was 'Tan tan tan'. He could have been famous but his doctor took the glory. I'm telling you to remember to write things down.

After that it was like a gold rush. Everyone started to open everyone's heads to find out what part was responsible for what. They all wanted to get a piece of the action and name some real estate in the brain after themselves. It has never been a dream of mine to have a tumour named after me, but the next guy to get famous on discovering a lesion was Wernicke who, in 1876, found an area below the Broca's area and he claimed that damage to this area was why one of his patients (another dead guy) couldn't string words together. He knew the words but could not create a sentence that made sense. So his patient would say 'catfoodgaloshesheadmake-cakeonmyhands'. Obviously, he couldn't argue with Wernicke so this area became known as Wernicke's area. To recap, Broca was the discoverer of the 'no speech' area and Wernicke was in charge of the 'not being able to string a sentence together' zone. It's a good thing the two patients never met. It would have been a dull party. Tan: 'Tan tan tan.' Wernicke's patient: 'What I understand you don't cow.' Tan: 'Tan tan tan.' Wernicke guy: 'You no gobble in paramedic horse me.' It would have been endless.

From this, neuroanatomists went into a frenzy and found that right across the top of our brain, from ear to ear, all humans have a somatosensory cortex where the brain receives signals from points on the surface of the body and registers them as touch. God knows how they found this thing out. I don't even want to know, but this is where the brain registers the sensation from every part of the body. So if you stuck a pin in the area in your brain that represents your third toe you would feel pain in your third toe. In this somatosensory cortex there is a whole map of every region of your body not in the order of your parts from your head to your toes, but rather in order of what areas are the most sensitive.

This goes for every single area on your skin: an elbow area, thumb area and genital area all have plots of real estate up in this somatic cortex where they can be felt. The size of the area relates to how many nerves you have in the specific region; the genital area and land of tongue are huge, because they are highly sensitized, while elbowville is not so huge. The county of shoulder – teeny. It's as if your body parts are getting bigger plots if they're used; genitals and tongue the size of Texas, armpit is Chattanooga.

★

If you had your foot amputated, you would still feel it in the foot neighbourhood of your brain which is a syndrome known as 'phantom limb'. And if certain parts of you are injured or diseased neurons will grow to compensate for the missing part. What I love most is the fact that in the somatic cortex, because the areas for the genitals are near the area for the feet, some people have reported that they feel they're having an orgasm in the area of a missing foot. Once these discoveries about the brain's wiring were made, all such bizarre syndromes started to make sense.

After this, neuroanatomists found and investigated movement maps of the brain. One such map was the motor cortex, which runs from one ear to the other over the top of your brain, like headphones, and each point controls a different part of the body. So rather than receive incoming sensations like in the somatosensory cortex, the motor cortex sends signals out, telling certain areas to move. If you stick a pin in the motor cortex area for your knee, your knee will twitch. If you stick the pin in the hip zone, the hip twitches; it may be possible to stick pins in certain parts of someone's head and make them walk like a chicken.

But back to science. It was also discovered that if you stuck a pin in one area of a person's cortex and his finger twitched, if you then stuck a pin in the exact area of another person's motor cortex, his finger might not twitch but his lip would. This is proof that each person is not created equally. Your cortical maps are all different sizes depending on which part of your body you use the most and the least; the more developed parts have larger corresponding brain regions.

The man who discovered this was a real hero of neuroplasticity: Michael Merzenich, a post-doctorate fellow at the University of Wisconsin-Madison.

He found that if you're a pianist and you practise moving your fingers up and down scales, hour after hour, day and night, more neurons would grow in the motor cortex of the finger area of the brain and expand its topography. I used to have a piano teacher who slammed the lid down while I was playing if I made a mistake, which is probably why I confess to war crimes when I see a piano. If you were a flamenco dancer you'd have more real estate in your toe area of your brain. Someone who licked stamps for a living would obviously have a larger tongue terrain. Do you see where I'm going with this?

When you're building up clusters of neurons by habitually moving certain parts of your body, it's like building muscles when you pump iron. In both cases the movement gets easier and more automatic because that area gets stronger. Of course, neural exercise doesn't give you bigger pecs or a six-pack hence the expression 'brain or brawn'. Many females choose brawn because it makes men look better in low-cut jeans and no top and some woman find that interesting; on the other hand, by building up thick neural clusters from all the finger work, Beethoven became a god of the ivories but not so big with the ladies.

What's Going on in Your Mind?

First let me say we've come such a long way from where we started. From a one-celled amoeba, a tiny pinheaded thing clinging onto a rock, to an evolutionary orchestrated master-piece; our brain, which looks like a three-pound piece of tofu. This jelly-like substance has more horsepower than every supercomputer that ever was squared. It has two hemispheres and various lobes that each play a crucial role. Zapping

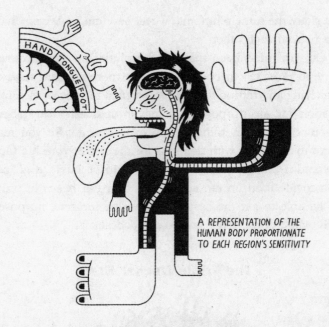

A REPRESENTATION OF THE HUMAN BODY PROPORTIONATE TO EACH REGION'S SENSITIVITY

throughout our inner landscape are approximately 100 billion neurons, electrically transmitting information, sending it at the speed of light throughout our whole nervous system. These 100 billion neurons can have anything from 10,000 to 100,000 branches or dendrites or connections (for the less bright) and every time you learn and experience something, they get better at firing and the wiring gets denser creating a SERIOUS FOREST OF BRAIN POWER. I have heard it said that the brain is capable of more connections than there are stars in the universe (how they counted this I have no idea and maybe they're making it up). It's hard to believe that each and every one of us carries this equipment, even Kim Kardashian. What a waste.

And yet we still have many glitches, we are not *homo perfectus* yet, far from it. We all basically have similar problems since we share the same plumbing. We all have cracks. We just hide them from each other.

Our brain has been shaped by evolutionary pressure over time to provide our bodies with ever more efficient ways of surviving and reproducing. It is designed to process all information for the purpose of living on, it doesn't care about happiness – it has things to do, places to go. So you may want to just swim with dolphins for the rest of your life (and some do) but most of us are primed to be busy; to go get, to provide food on tap and a roof over our heads in order to be able to get the best mate possible for gene purposes. (Google 'trophy wives' and 'sugar daddies'.)

The Triple-Decker Brain

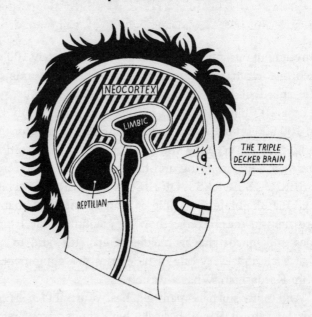

The cause of much of our confusion is that we actually have too many brains in our heads: three to be precise. Starting with the oldest brain, the other two newer ones are outside it like Russian dolls; a brain within a brain within a brain. Unfortunately our old reptilian brain didn't get absorbed, it's still in there squashed with the newer models, like a relative you can't get rid of.

This ancient brain, developed about 400 million years ago, is called the brain stem; it is the 'duh' part of the brain. It prompts us to mate, kill and eat, which is perfect if you're living in a field or working at Goldman Sachs.

Then around 250 million years ago, the paleomammalian brain (but that's way too long a word) or limbic system came on-line; that's where we, unlike reptiles, were motivated to bond with and nurture our offspring, rather than eat them. (Not such a bad idea when you think about school fees.)

During our neomammalian phase, about 500,000 years ago, we grew a superior brain, the prefrontal cortex; the executive brain, El Capitano. This provided us with the tools for self-control, consciousness, awareness, language and self-regulation. Also for rational, strategic and logical thought, math and morality. It is the gatekeeper to the primitive brain, so if you suddenly want to eat without a fork, it will inform you that it isn't such a good idea. Same with going to the loo in public. The brain tripled in size in the last three million years (which of course is a blink in the history of us) and we suddenly got the ability to feel sorry for each other and acquired cooperation skills like group hugging (see New Age).

This mish mash of three brains, called the lizard-squirrel-monkey brain, all trying to function at once is one reason why we're nuts. This is why there are women who read Heidegger but also want to screw the plumber.

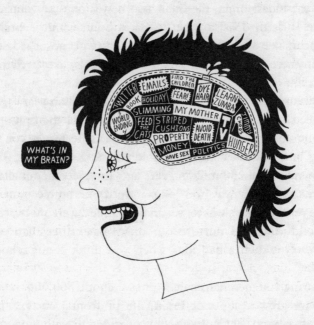

I'd like to mention President Clinton as an example of how confused we are; a man who could run a country but could not for the life of him stop himself from inserting a cigar in one of the most inappropriate places on Earth. There are no matches or lighters in there, whatever he says.

I will explain where things may have started to go wrong for us: errors thanks to evolution. Millions of years ago, when we were ancient man, as I have said, we were perfectly fine and at one with our environment (no one had panic attacks or OCD). When we met a predator and felt danger or threat, we'd fill up with our own adrenaline and cortisol to take on our foe. Kill or be killed. Have lunch or be lunch. After the ordeal was over, we'd defuel and the chemicals would go back to normal.

The problem these days as modern man is that when we perceive danger, adrenaline shoots into us but because we can't kill a traffic warden or eat an estate agent, the juice never comes back down. We're in a constant state of red light alert, like a car siren that drives you nuts.

Because we can't kill people who anger us, we have all this pent-up rage. To make things worse when language came on-line about 70,000 years ago we started to use words to describe those constant feelings of alarm so everything was perceived as an emergency. Now, it wasn't just, 'Oh, there's a sabre tooth tiger', it was, 'Oh, I forgot to send that email', 'Everyone hates me', 'My thighs are too fat', 'I didn't get invited to the Christmas party'. This is what drives us mad: the never-ending voices.

The thing that helped us survive in the past (our alarm system) now gives us nervous breakdowns. Someone said, 'Man was built for survival, not for happiness'. Sorry to be the bearer of bad news but our pets are happier than us. So cats, happy happy. Dogs, happy happy. Human beings, screwed. Completely screwed.

A Little About Stress

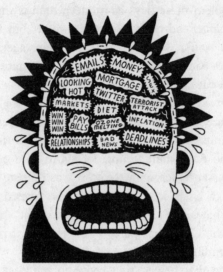

THE STRESSED BRAIN

These days we are more likely to die in different ways from our ancestors. We (in the West) no longer have to worry about scarlet fever, bubonic plague or cholera. In the 1900s, the big diseases were tuberculosis, pneumonia and influenza. A person living through the First World War was more likely to die of flu or pneumonia than in battle. Now because we're living longer and better than ever before, we slowly fall apart.

Out on the Savannah, our physiological responses were perfectly suited to deal with stressors (run from the big animals with big teeth). These days we can't just run from what drives up our anxiety and stress; mortgages, money problems, looking hot, relationships and deadlines. Evolution did not set us up to suffer Jurassic Park levels of stress, day in day out; that's the bitch of living at today's pace.

What's in Your Brain/What's on Your Mind?

Psychological stress is a fairly new concept. People might say, 'Oh, come on you lightweight, we can deal with stress, bring it on.' It isn't the stress that makes you sick or even your risk of being sick. Stress increases your risk of getting diseases that make you sick, or if you're already sick and you add stress, you can kiss farewell to your natural defences. The fact we can't switch off our alarm is what makes us vulnerable. So here's my point: stress-related diseases are disorders of excessive stress responses. (Take it or leave it).

As I said before, you can be the creator of your own stress without any outside influence. As soon as you even think about stress, a whole cascade of reactions happen: your thalamus (the relay station of your brain) sends out a wake-up call to your brain stem, signals are sent to all your major organs and muscle groups getting them ready for fight or flight and your adrenal glands release the stress hormones; cortisol suppresses the immune system to reduce inflammation from any injuries and stimulates the amygdala to keep you vigilant, which produces even more cortisol. It also suppresses activity in the hippocampus reducing your memory so you only think about what you did last time you had a similar emergency. This chemical also stops your digestion and the urge to have sex. (Unless you have a weird quirk – there are some people who like to have sex during a hurricane). Thinking about sex or eating during a disaster would only make things worse. Another chemical, epinephrine, increases your heartbeat so it can move more blood and dilates your pupils (to help you find your foe in the dark). All this is useful if you're actually in danger. If you're not actually in a life or death situation and those chemicals can't stop pumping through you, they will wreak havoc on your body and brain. They will kill off neurons in the hippocampus creating permanent memory loss. Oxygen and blood flood to your peripheries to get your arms and legs ready to kick ass but if they stay there too long, your brain gets depleted of air and fresh blood so your thinking goes down; intelligence may become a thing of the past and you might wake up (or actually not wake) to find yourself in a coma.

Excessive chemicals eventually inhibit your immune system (the defence against infections and illnesses) making you vulnerable to viruses of every shape and size. They will lower the production of serotonin (making you feel listless and joyless as in depression) and can eventually, if they remain virulent, cause heart disease, hardening of the arteries, type 2 diabetes and certain cancers. Inadvertently stress will destroy you both mentally and physically unless you change the way you think about it and relate to it.

With mindfulness, you learn to regulate these chemicals, intentionally increasing the ones that promote health and happiness and decreasing the ones that don't.

My Story

As someone who suffers from depression, I decided to take up mindfulness as an antidote to this very harmful build-up of cortisol. We can't get rid of stress so this practice is a way I learnt to deal with it. When my emotions get too high, whether it's elation or distress, I have to come back to a baseline or I'll literally be flooded by my own cortisol and swept away by depression. Because I've had so many episodes, I only need a few drops of this toxic chemical and I'm vulnerable to its effects. Before doing a show, I have to use mindfulness practices (see later in Part 4) to cool my engine so that I can take the hit of adrenaline that comes with the job and use it to my advantage. If I'm too 'up' on stage I'm anything but funny, I become a desperate woman with those pleading, fear-filled eyes. I know myself better these days and can only succeed if I work from a level of calm to make creative thinking possible otherwise my head fills with the 'everyone hates me' school of thought. If I'm calm, I can think on my feet, my eyes lose their desperation, and creativity flows. This doesn't mean I'm in a 'blah' state, it just means I'm keeping my eye on my speedometer so I can step on the brake or accelerate when I need to. For me this is done with mindfulness not wishful thinking.

Parts of the Brains –
The Easy-to-Understand Version

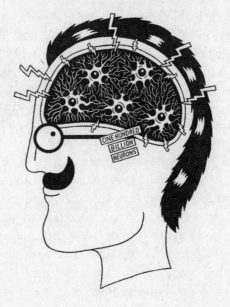

'Let's start at the very beginning, a very good place to start.' I like to quote Julie Andrews when discussing neuroscience. The pattern of how neurons or cells are wired together determines the way we think. Whatever we experience mentally is a result of the different combinations of neurons. As I said earlier, each neuron can link up with 10,000 to 100,000 neighbours and make connections. The parts that join up are branches or dendrites (which receive incoming information) and axons (which send signals).

The inside of your head could be compared to Las Vegas, where every experience, sensation, thought and feeling corresponds with billions of electrical lights zapping on and off like a Mexican hand wave on a gigantic electric grid. Your ability to do everything, including your dreams, hopes, fantasies, fears and most of all your ability to read this book, is created by neuronal connections, chemicals and specialized regions in your brain calibrated by your genetic history, your development, the society you're born into and of course, Mommy and Daddy.

Neurons transmit information to each other via electrical impulses not dissimilar to those used to jolt Frankenstein up from the gurney and make him kill people. When a neuron fires, an electrochemical wave ripples through it, on its way to signalling the next neuron.

You may have learnt this at school but I will remind you that the neurons don't actually touch each other, between each of them is a tiny gap, called a synapse, between which chemicals are passed called neurotransmitters. When neurons become excited through enough stimulation (because of a thought or experience) an electrical wavelet fires down the length of the cell to activate or inhibit the neurotransmitters. At the other side of each gap are little receptors, like flowers opening to pass the chemicals across the synaptic cleft and lodge in the next neuron. Once they cross over they create an electrical zap that sends an electrical message to the next neuron. This is how neurons communicate with each other through electrical and chemical impulses and those babies can go from speeds of two to 20 miles per hour. The whole process is not dissimilar to pass the parcel but it's electric. (This game would kill children). Just think, all this is going on inside your brain, right now and you're just lying there without knowing it. You should get on your knees and thank evolution.

Learning is about new neurons connecting together; memory is made possible by those changes happening over

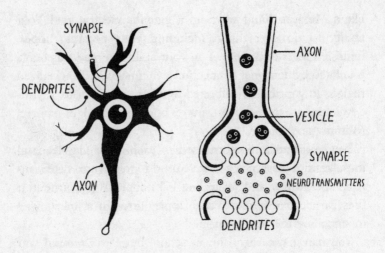

many times because you're memorizing a new fact and you study it again and again, your synapses are actually changing their shape to speed up receptiveness and increase the firing, making them more efficient at passing information in the future. Learning has happened because of the synapse changing shape and the longer the shape is retained, the longer you hold that information. USE IT OR LOSE IT. If you repeat a mode of thinking or behaving, the pattern of the neurons becomes strengthened. NEURONS THAT FIRE TOGETHER, WIRE TOGETHER. When they don't fire, the connections eventually just shrivel and die just like the Wicked Witch of the West melted in *The Wizard of Oz* when they threw water on her.

Your average neuron fires 5 to 50 times a second, meaning there are zillions and zillions of signals travelling inside your head right now carrying snippets of information. The nervous system moves information exactly like your heart moves blood. All those zillions of emails zapping around in your head are what define the mind, most of which you will never be aware of. The number of possible combinations of 100 billion neurons firing or not firing is ten to the millionth power, or one followed by a million zeros. (I'm just trying to show you there's a lot going on in your head.)

As more and more complex skills became part of your repertoire, from rubbing sticks to make fire to building a rocket, more and more neural cells connect and grow and these dendrites or connections become stronger and stronger and more and more synchronized in their firing patterns. If you learnt Mandarin, you'd get a whole set of synchronized neurons in the language department or if you take up banjo a whole bunch of neurons are lighting up in your brain in your finger area on the somatic map in your brain. Whatever you're using or thinking about is reflected in areas lighting up in your brain and you can watch this firework display during brain scanning.

Everything that happens, every thought, feeling and perception you have, changes your brain and those changes are how you learn things, from bowling to dumping your boyfriend. However, the brain isn't just a mass of unspecialized information processors, it has certain regions that do certain jobs.

Neurons (with their shooting neurotransmitters) form into pathways and multiple networks with specialized functions and via these pathways the regions are able to communicate with each other; the way a tube system works going from station to station. All information processed by the brain is nothing more than electricity passing through neuron after neuron with little squirts of juice across their gaps. (If you're a religious person this might upset you.)

Genes

I can hear you ask, 'What about genes? Don't they play a part in all this?' No one knows how much your genes contribute to make you who you are or how much your experience shapes you. Nature (referring to genes a person has inherited) or nurture (influenced by environmental factors)? It's a toss-up. Genes hand you a deck of cards; how you play them is up to you. A gene is a unit of hereditary information linked to one or more physical traits; leg length (I'm furious I will never go down the catwalk with what I've got), blonde hair (another thing I wished I had), and larger lips (a must for my modelling career). Your genetic code (the blueprint of you) is contained in your DNA and informs each and every cell where to go (which is why your ear doesn't grow out of your foot) so your DNA is like a traffic warden directing trillions of cells, determining what each cell actually becomes and killing off those that make a wrong turn.

Genes create proteins and they can turn that gene expression on and off, up and down. In the brain, gene expression influences levels of neurotransmitters, which influence functions like intelligence. This is why some people get As without working for them (I hate them). Or they influence memory; for those who win quiz shows about general knowledge (I hate them).

The environment also influences gene expression, so how your brain works and who you become depends on diet, education and the colour of your wallpaper.

We have around 31,000 genes and they don't all get switched on, no matter what Mommy and Daddy passed. Good news for those of you with crazy parents. You might be just fine, depending on your experiences. Some behaviour is more heritable than others; you may start off with some genes loaded for depression but they don't just switch on without some environmental input. No one knows if you become 'you' because of nature or nurture: it's a combination of what you're born with and how you live your life.

In our early years we are vulnerable to bad environmental experiences so Mommy and Daddy can seriously damage your gene expression. Each baby is, in the first five years of its life, at the mercy of its parents' download . . . and they got their downloads from their parents . . . and all the way back to the baboon and beyond. (It's a miracle we're not still swinging from trees. Next time you see royalty, just picture their forefathers squatting in the bush.)

The brain is divided into four lobes. Form has function and I'm going to tell you about it, at least all that I know.

Just a note, the brain is much, much more complicated than my humble descriptions; many regions overlap in their functions and cognitive neuroscientists spend their days figuring out what each of the specific regions do. In a way, they're still in the dark and so am I. The following is just a broad sketch – so if you're a neuroscientist don't bite my head off or any one of my lobes.

Four Lobes –
Each Lobe Has a Right and Left Side

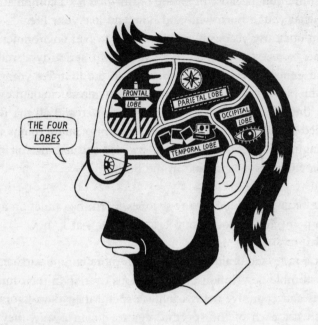

Occipital Lobe

Responsible for most of our visual processing. We don't actually see the world through our eyeballs, instead the light shines through the retina and sends projections to different groups of neurons in the occipital lobe each specialized to interpret various components of visual information, for example:

Colour
Orientation
Shape
Light and shade
Face-recognition

This lobe works in conjunction with other regions (parietal and temporal lobes) that are organized into streams of visual information, such as the 'what' pathway determining if it's a chair, cow or your mother and a 'where' pathway telling you, in your house, in the yard, on your face.

So contrary to popular belief, it's not your actual eyeball that sees the world, you have a whole production company in the back of your head beavering away, producing a movie; creating the illusion that what you see is reality. It's a film called *Reality* rather than actual reality. So many things are going on back there in the occipital and this is how you can remember a face or a scene and say, 'Oh yes, I remember who you are, didn't I marry you ten years ago?' – something I've been known to say to my husband.

Temporal Lobe

Located around the ears and besides giving you surround-sound (auditory perception) it retains your visual memories (including faces), provides you with your ability to comprehend language and meaning (hello existentialists), carries out emotional processing (in the amygdala) and is the home of specialized 'explicit memory' centres such as the hippocampus. When there's a strong emotion during an experience, chances are you won't forget it thanks to structures in your temporal lobe: say on your tenth birthday, you saw a horse fall off a cliff and you became hysterical, that magic photo opportunity will be locked in your long-term memory for life. Emotional memories stick the longest. That's why when you're memorizing history in school, you should picture yourself in the Battle of Hastings and pretend to lose your legs. You won't forget it then.

Parietal Lobe

Integrates sensory and visual information, so you can navigate with a sort of internal compass to tell you where you are in space and give you a sense of being in your body. It then coordinates your movements in response to objects and tells you where and what they are, constantly updating the information as you move and interact with the world. This navigation system is a must to stop you from crashing into the furniture.

Frontal Lobe

The largest of the brain's structures. It is what makes (most of) us civilized and creates our personalities; it is the big boy of mental ability. This is the seat of our emotions and allows us to understand how someone else is thinking and feeling. It can plan a whole scenario so we can rehearse an outcome before we initiate it. Among its list of accolades are some of these babies:

Decision-making
Problem-solving
Emotional impulsivity
Judgment
And best of all, impulse control or self-regulation

Right and Left Brain

Corpus Callosum

The two hemispheres are connected by a bridge made of a densely packed band of nerve fibres shunting information back and forth, facilitating a continuous dialogue between the two halves; if this didn't exist your left side wouldn't know what your right side was doing (and could play very cruel tricks on it). Luckily, it can seamlessly create the illusion that you are the result of one brain rather than two. Each hemisphere controls the movement in the opposite side of the body.

Contrary to popular myth, the right brain is not just the female feeling part of the brain and the left, the macho business side. It's more complicated than simple ladies and men signs on restroom doors: these two sides took hundreds of millions of years to develop and evolution wouldn't come up with something that flimsy. The two sides share many features and yet at the same time each side has specialized processing systems. Each side seems to compensate in strength for what the other lacks. The right isn't good at grammar so the left is sensational. The right is touchy-feely to get the big picture while the left is better at reading, writing and doing arithmetic and sweats about the details.

Perhaps from early in our evolution one side had to have narrow focus to find food (left) while the other side (right) had to be on the look-out, vigilant at watching out in case we were jumped.

Some Skills of the Right Side

Not great at grammar or vocabulary but fantastic at picking up intonation and accent

Creative

Intuitive

Skilled at putting pieces together (great at puzzles)

The home of autobiographical memory – the story of you

Picks up metaphors and jokes.

All the information from the right is then sent to Lefty for interpretation.

Some Skills of the Left Side

Linear

Logical

Able to plan

Accurate and able to think literally and retrieve facts

In charge of vocabulary

It's the area responsible for those internal voices (boo hiss)

The narrator of your on-going personal life story

The region where list-making lurks (boo hiss).

The left side is more densely woven with closely-packed neurons, making this side better at doing intense, detailed work. These left-brainers are brilliant but can be very boring people. If there's too much left-brain, analytical and logical thinking, you may not be a very warm and cosy individual. They make great businessmen but not always great guys. Asperger's-like symptoms are a big advantage for these folks who need to focus on one particular thing and everything else can go to hell. Some people think this gift of pin-sized focus as seen in autism is a must for the information age. Left-brainers can sit for hours staring at a screen and nothing outside interferes; like a life.

Also it's believed that because men had to figure out how to make a spear back in the old days, they probably began to carry the autism gene because who would want to spend a lifetime wittling away at a stone? Certainly not a woman.

The ideal is if the two hemispheres work together they make a perfect couple i.e. if the right gets a vibe that there is something dangerous outside then the left defines what it is. Creating a coherent narrative of your own life story involves the integration of the two hemispheres. Too much in the left you've got a boring accountant or Bill Gates, too much in the right you get someone who talks to angels and probably can't do math.

Parts of the Brain – Part Two

Right under the corpus callosum is the limbic system, the more ancient mammalian part of the brain. This part is good news for survival and motivation, bad news for civilization. Too much reaction from the limbic and not enough prefrontal cortex keeping you in check, and you may turn out to be a thug or a junkie.

A Few Parts in the Limbic System

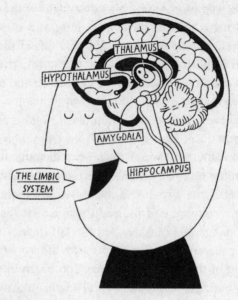

Hypothalamus

Involved with the translation of conscious experience into bodily processes; you think, then you move. It's also involved with the part where behaviour influences hormones. Here are a few of the processes controlled by the hypothalamus:

Hunger
Thirst
Body temperature
Sexuality
Blood pressure
Sleep

What's in Your Brain/What's on Your Mind?

Thalamus

Sends a wake-up call to the brain stem (the 'duh' part of the brain) sending signals to all major organs and muscle groups; like a call centre that redirects incoming traffic to the appropriate area and if need be gets you ready to rumble or run. All sensory information (except smell) is passed and processed through the thalamus. It's thought to be involved in consciousness because if you lose power there, you'll find yourself in a coma.

Hippocampus

Shaped like a seahorse, it works like a search engine to locate and retrieve other memories quickly and smoothly like a great secretary who knows where all your life is filed away.

Amygdala

The emergency alarm of the brain sending responses to various parts of the body from emotionally relevant information. It coordinates physiological responses to get you ready to fight or run and makes sure you remember it.

A Few Parts in the Frontal Lobe

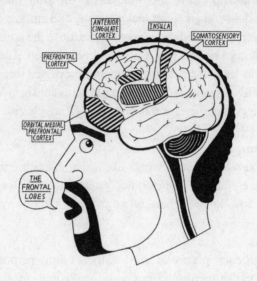

Prefrontal Cortex

The 'higher part' of the brain. Helps with assessing and choosing the correct social behavior (it's the 'pinky up' part of the brain when you have tea at the Ritz) and has numerous other talents:

Higher thinking
Planning
Reasoning
Judging
Self-regulation
Impulse control

Anterior Cingulate Cortex

The overseer of attention. It monitors predictive errors and conflicts such as the distance you are from your goals. It is the basis of working memory; a workspace where you can gather information and solve problems and make decisions. It's also where actions are planned. The ACC comes into its own when you:

Gather information
Solve problems
Make decisions
Plan actions
Fulfill your intentions
Self-regulate

The ACC doesn't develop until you're between three and six years old; this is probably why kids have hissy fits.

Orbital Medial Prefrontal Cortex
Regulates information from the external and internal worlds especially in relation to reward. Its inhibition function can say, 'Whoa boy', to the amygdala before it sends out the full alarm to 'kill or run' or other embarrassingly primitive reactions, such as defecating on the carpet or having sex in an elevator. Using these reins makes you polite even when you want to chew someone's head off.

Somatosensory Cortex
As mentioned before, a region in the brain that has a map of all your body parts. The map isn't in order from your toes, knees, thighs up to your head. It's in the order of which parts are the most sensitive so the lips are right next to the genitals (an anatomical joke).

Insula

Gives you all those internal 'vibes', so the feeling of butter-flies flapping their wings in your stomach or knives in your heart. This area gives you a visceral weather report from inside. If you sense these feelings and link them with the ACC, you can then reflect on them and consciously make a decision if you want to pull the reins or not. (I'll be discussing this later because the ACC is responsible for self-awareness and regulation that are strengthened by the practice of mindfulness.)

Cerebellum

The 'small brain' at the tail end of the big brain leading to the spine; in charge of balance, posture and coordination.

Basal Ganglia

An area involved in motivation, motor selection and action. It controls everything from big muscle movements to the flicker of the eyes caused by surprise, novelty, cravings or drive. It uses our memories and translates them into motiva-tion and then action. If it were to be removed, you'd be more like a doormat.

The Chemicals That Make You Who You Are

You know the expression, 'it's just the hormones talking'? This is usually said in a derogatory way to women who are having their period. Just because I have threatened people with a buzz saw through their car at this time of the month, I am categorized as hormonal. But 'ha ha', it's not just us.

Men, children, even pets are at the mercy of the hormones that dictate their moods. When you fall in love, it's not because someone sprayed fairy dust on you, it's just a hormone within that has been switched on. It gets complicated, but to give you an idea, when a thought occurs it sends a message to your thalamus which emails the pituitary gland which in turn phones the adrenal which sends hormones responding to the original thought. Maybe we're all just different recipes; recipes with legs. When someone asks how you are, you should just hand him or her a list of your ingredients. This is far more accurate than a star sign if you ask me.

Here are some of those ingredients and their main functions. There are more than one hundred different agents known to serve as neurotransmitters and many of these have different functions in different regions of the brain.

Serotonin
The feel-good chemical, it increases energy levels and regulates sleep and digestion. Most anti-depressants aim at increasing its effects. You really want this chemical or life just isn't worth living. Obviously, you can buy it over the counter as an anti-depressant so you don't have to suck it out of a friend's neck if you're low on it. It can turn anxiety into serenity and optimism but also affects other areas: appetite, blood pressure and pain levels.

Dopamine
As I've said, motivates you to seek rewards. Cocaine does the same thing but it's more expensive. It switches on (the basal ganglia lets you know you're running low) when you anticipate getting what you want, which is why the chase tastes

better than the kill; it lights up under the scanner when we know we're just about to get our object of desire. Experiments on rats have shown that they'll give up food, sex and rock and roll just to get a hit of dopamine. That's how good it feels and rats are no fools.

Those driven, ambitious, A-type personalities are high on (among other things) their own dopamine, so they keep it on a constant drip always seeking situations that jack it up a notch.

Noradrenaline

Also called 'norepinephrine'. Influences sleep and attention; it excites, alerts and arouses. This is your 'get up and go' hit. It starts your heart racing and blood rushing but too much of this and you find yourself in flighting or fighting mode. When a squirrel lifts its little head and jerks it around to look for trouble, he's on norepinephrine.

Acetylocholine

A shot of this would make you whizz through university exams; it promotes attention, learning, memory and neuro-plasticity and is critical for control of muscles by motor neurons (it keeps your heart pumping so you don't want to go to empty on this chemical). Near the brain stem, when this chemical is released it enables neurons that are activated to strengthen their connections to one another.

Endorphine

Reduces pain and stress and creates a sense of 'whoopy' by suppressing shame, vigilance and self-criticism so now you can dance on table tops in your underwear with a flower in your nose.

Oxytocin

When this switches on you'll feel all cosy and milky like the perfect mommy. Very important to have while raising children; without it you'll want to flush them away when they make noise. If you reach out and touch someone, your oxytocin is lactating. Those with a lot of oxytocin could be described as cuddly, wanting to take care and metaphorically breastfeed everyone. In the queue of life they're always at the back taking care of others. (I have very little of this drug.)

Glutamate

The brain's CEO as far as exciting the neurotransmitters and forging links between neurons via the synapses. It's the most stimulating neurotransmitter for learning because it changes the way synapses work thereby making it easier and more likely for them to fire. The more they fire the more engrained new knowledge becomes. The parts of the brain that use glutamate to communicate the most are the cortex and the hippocampus. Take out the hippocampus (a scientist did this by accident to some guy) and you have around a 30-second memory. (See goldfish.) No glutamate and you can't lay down any new memories at all. Knock out the genes for glutamate receptors in mice and you get mice who will never find the cheese again. (I'm not suggesting you really do that.) If you give mice more glutamate receptors you get 'super mice' that are going for their PhDs.

Vasopressin

Supports pair bonding, attachment and monogamy. It decreases aggressiveness in males and turns them into caretaking and intimacy-seeking creatures who write Valentine's Day cards and stay faithful. We should put vasopressin in their food.

Testosterone

Those who habitually fill up with testosterone literally have no brain. It's a no-brainer; a lot of sex but no brain.

Cortisol

I talked about this one before, it is your friend and foe; it can get you going, put a tiger in your tank or debilitate you.

As I mentioned, things are much more complex than I've described because these chemicals affect you in different ways depending on where in the brain they're switched on. For example, Parkinson patients have too little dopamine in an area of the brain that controls movement. If you increase their dopamine, the shaking stops but now there's too much dopamine in other parts of the brain so you've got a guy who's suddenly addicted to gambling or sex. Now he's not shaking but he's broke and a pervert. You see the problem? For depression it's not as simple as increasing your serotonin because if you pump it in, it's like cluster-bombing; what's affective in one area may damage the next. Neuroscientists are still in the dark about anti-depressants because how can they research what happens to neurons when there are hundreds of billions of them? (Like finding your contact lens in the Sahara.)

Memory

Here's where knowledge of the brain gets fuzzy: around memory. Neuroscientists are unable to localize where memory is in the brain; it seems it's everywhere. If the amygdala is persistently stimulated or there's a big enough shock, the synapses change shape making them more sensitive to fear stimuli and you'll feel fear faster next time something similar happens to scare you. If the motor cortex is stimulated enough by firing neurons in that region you'll learn the skills to whack a tennis ball or snow ski. Pain is learnt through over-stimulated neurons in the somatic cortex so, by merely touching something, the sensation is more easily triggered, magnifying the agony. So memory is the result of long-term potentiation causing the neurons to be more readily fired.

Most of the understanding about memory comes from either brain accidents or traumas. There was a guy called H.M. who, when he was nine-years-old, fell off his bike. He was fine for a while but by 25 he started having severe seizures. To find a way to alleviate these episodes, the surgeon took out both the right and left sides of his hippocampus; no one had ever done that. He seemed fine but for a tiny problem; whatever he did he couldn't remember that he had done it before. He'd eat and not know it and eat again. Each time he met someone it was as if it was the first time. (No short-term memory.) If you were a comedian this man would be your ideal audience. It became clear that you need your hippocampus to convert short-term memory into long-term memory. What was amazing was that he could remember everything before the accident so his long-term memory was intact. Clearly memory is stored in other parts of the brain.

There are two major kinds of memory processes; explicit and implicit:

Explicit Memory
Stored in the hippocampus and medial temporal cortex for facts, events, people and places. You need to make a

conscious effort to recall these memories, eg when was your first kiss and where? For me it was in my closet with God knows who . . . I was stoned. (I hope it was a person and not a shoe.)

Implicit Memory

These are unconscious memories: when you learn to ride a bike you're firing off clusters of neurons that help you pedal and balance, and every detail becomes automatic so you don't have to think back to remember them. Implicit memory is stored in various places in the brain; movement is stored in the motor cortex and cerebellum and the memory of certain emotions is stored in the amygdala.

For the first 18 months of our lives we only encode implicit memory: smells, tastes, sounds; bodily and emotional sensations. The brain combines similar events and constructs mental models from repeated events. If Mommy hugged you repeatedly during childhood, you'd start to expect it whenever you saw her. This information is then embedded in your synaptic connections, which ultimately shape your brain so whenever you see Mommy or someone who looks like her, you're 'primed' to expect that hug. (I find these people particularly irritating and, even worse, they want a hug back. I am going to make a t-shirt that says 'No Hugs'.)

Your hippocampus pulls together separate images and sensations from implicit memory, like pieces of a puzzle, into pictures of factual and autobiographical material.

In order to couple the detail of an experience with an emotional kick, the hippocampus has to work with other limbic areas like the amygdala – this is why you'll never forget the smell of the sea on the night your boyfriend threw you off a cliff.

When images and sensations stay in implicit memory and aren't integrated by the hippocampus they remain disconnected with the past. This could explain the way you have flashbacks from traumatic experiences because you can't identify the fear and panic as belonging to the past.

Autobiographical Memory

As time goes on, you collect and condense more and more episodic memories into larger files along a time-line. At this point you can start to tell funny or sad stories about different times in your life, compare various experiences and create a narrative. As you elaborate these multiple episodes you eventually have yourself an autobiography; now you can write a book about the story of your life (if anyone will buy it).

How Memory Works

The mind is always recording whether you're awake or asleep. We sometimes dip into our consciousness and maybe pick out a few random words or snippets of thought and embroider them together to form a tale. This random fishing in thoughts does not actually reveal who you are. I apologize to any Freudians reading this but scrutinizing the minutiae of your thoughts is like studying your faeces through a microscope. If you learn about yourself from that, good luck to you.

Whenever you use memory, you're retrieving it from storage in the various parts of your brain working together to create the remembered event. It uses the emotional impact: your fear, joy or shame, to colour how you'll remember something. The image is imprinted by what you felt. Also your feelings in a situation will be as different from the next person as your fingerprint. This is why so many people remember the scene of the crime differently. We are all biased in terms of how we bring up the past. Each time a memory is recalled, it is an amalgamation from various sections of the brain. If you call it up again and again you get versions of old versions like an elaborate Chinese whisper and each time it becomes more distorted.

Our brains collect images from the moment we're born and file them away as either safe or dangerous. Whenever we see someone or something we dive into our memories to see who that person or scene reminds us of. In our visual cortex there is a region for face recognition. Its job is comparing who's in front of you with faces you recall from the past. All of this happens in a billionth of a second and is under the radar so we don't realize how biased our judgment is when we meet a new person, making racists, bigots and sexist pigs of us all. So if I meet a slightly obese, older woman with dyed red hair and wire-rimmed glasses, I will probably be hostile because my grandmother looked like that and always took out her false teeth in front of my friends. This poor woman won't know why I'm treating her like a leper.

The whole brain works as a unit to keep you alive. Isn't that heartwarming? Someone cares. You. Each of these parts of your brain individually wouldn't know what to do and would be just a lump of uselessness but all together they are more complex then the universe and beyond (See *Star Trek*).

If, say, you're walking in the jungle and there's a curvy thing on the ground. In the first few tenths of a second light bounces off the curvy thing and is sent to the occipital cortex where it's registered, then for further processing the image is sent to the hippocampus (the filing cabinet) to evaluate if it's a threat or an opportunity. If the hippocampus gets a slight feeling this squiggly thing could be dangerous it sends out a 'jump-now-check-later' message, which informs the amygdala that in turn rings the alarm, 'Emergency, emergency'. This warning notifies your fight or flight neural and hormonal systems and at that point your reproductive and digestive organs shut down because, as I've said, the last thing you need to do when you're about to be obliterated is to eat or have sex. Almost immediately, blood and oxygen drain from your brain to shoot into your arms and legs to get you ready for fight or flight. Your heart speeds up, your breathing accelerates. Your memory and any clear thinking are obliterated because all your glucose and blood have left the building and are heading out to your peripheries.

Meanwhile the slow prefrontal cortex has been yanking information out of long-term memory trying to figure out if it's a stick or a snake. It may register that no one else around has panicked and, after a few more seconds, access the neurons it needs to fire into the pattern that informs you it's a stick. How about that for teamwork? Eventually this experience works its way to the language centres but not until much later, so in the height of panic you have no words. They take about 240 milliseconds for you to even start a grunt. And then let the swearing begin.

How You Develop

Evolution plays its part in creating an experience-dependent brain in that you are born inside out (don't panic it all works out) so when you're only a one-month-old embryo, your outer layer of cells folds inward forming your brain stem and this is why our insides were once literally connected to the outside. The DNA instructs the neurons on which area they should migrate to. They then connect to each other, based on your experience and that ultimately will determine how your brain is shaped. Only the strong and often-used neurons survive and the rest die off, like sperm that don't make it through the big swim.

Somehow every single cell has to know if it's a cell for your nose or part of your toenail and find its way to that particular area. No satnav, no nothing. Can you imagine that kind of a challenge? Trillions of cells trying to put together the puzzle of all your parts; what makes you you. It would be like rush hour, squared. What are the chances that you come out vaguely normal and not looking like a Picasso with three breasts coming out of your forehead? I wouldn't bet on the odds. And let's say you form the full complement of limbs and digits and a brain that works, now you depend on your parents (two descendants of a one-celled amoeba) to fill your tiny empty brain with the first spoonfuls of knowledge; teaching you to talk, walk, think, feel, flirt and freak out. This is why each of us, each generation, has to struggle with this universal quandary: what are we supposed to be doing here?

How Our Brains Grow

Reptiles lay some eggs or just stand and deliver and move on; without sentimentality they walk away to mate again somewhere with anyone who happens to be mounting them at the time while they're munching on some lawn. Then the baby automatically knows how to swim, slither, trot or fly away. We are born knowing nothing and just lie there in our own mess till someone lifts us out of it and bothers to change our pants. They (animals) need no manual, they just know things. Compared to other primates, humans are born far too early for their brain to be mature. (If we could stay in our mother's womb for the brain to fully develop we'd be in there 24 months.) The only reason we come out at nine months is because our heads wouldn't fit through the birth canal if we stayed in there and would end up doing some serious damage to Mommy; she would probably never walk again and sue us for personal injury. You know that scene in *Ben Hur* where they tie each of a man's legs to an elephant and then scream, 'Giddy up'? That's how Mommy would feel.

The genes build the scaffolding of your head in-vitro but once outside Baby only has his basic amphibian brain, just enough to keep his heart and breathing going and that's about all. But it's not all bad news, evolution can be smart sometimes and because we come out so undercooked the development of our brain depends on external experience. We have so much to learn once we're out so we need that external stimuli to develop, which is a blessing because it would be impossible to learn shorthand or ping pong while we're inside the womb. This is a very clever idea because no one knows where you're going to be born and you need different skills depending on the area and culture you plop out into. If you're born in the Sahara, it would be good to have a structure that would make you proficient in camel straddling or if you're born in New York, it's more helpful if you develop the motor skills to honk and scream at other drivers. We have so much learning to do. (This is called *neural Darwinism*.)

By age three, the baby's brain has formed about 1000 trillion synaptic connections. At that point, the baby has the equipment to speak any language in the world. Its ears, tongue and mouth are primed for any sound or accent that may be needed depending on where it's born. The sounds around you shape your tongue and palate, so the first 16 months will determine your accent. If you are Chinese, you will probably leave out 'r's for the rest of your life. 'I'm sowwy but it's twoo'. If you're German, you will probably make that sound in your throat that sounds like you're about to bring up phlegm.

Before you learn to speak, your brain is like a wad of chewing gum so any language is possible to learn with the perfect accompanying accent and, unless you become an impressionist, you'll be stuck with it. You better learn fast at this point because after the first two months half your neurons drop dead.

The right hemisphere has a higher rate of growth during the first 18 months, which establish the basic structures of attachment and emotional regulation. During the second year of life, a growth spurt happens in the left hemisphere. We learn to crawl, then walk and then there's an explosion of language skills such as saying 'poo, poo'. The hands and eyes become more connected to visual stimuli and vocabulary develops, so now we can demand things like a rattle on ice with a splash of vermouth. The language areas are activated by about 18 months after birth and babies begin to develop self-consciousness where they can recognize themselves in a mirror. This is the birth of the concept of 'I' when you get that feeling that you are you, if you know what I mean.

As Baby matures, neural circuits guided by the environment, connect. As sensory systems develop, they provide increasingly precise input to shape neural network formation and more and more complex patterns of behaviour. Now Baby can draw like Rembrandt. Movements and emotional networks connect with motor systems so you can spit in someone's face because they have pissed you off. Now all the wires of behaviour, movement, sensory experience and emotions connect and feed each other information-like wires in a complex phone system. Right and left hemisphere integration allows us to put feelings into words. This linking up of right and left hemispheres is accomplished through Mommy and Baby eye contact, facial expressions and speaking 'goo goo' which is called 'motherese'. (Some lesbians use it with their cats.) The baby imitates Mommy and so she/he learns how to put feelings into words. Then when Mommy rocks the baby, her hormones are released making baby feel safe. A game of peek-a-boo activates the baby's nervous system by the fine art of surprise and leads to cascades of biological processes enhancing Baby's excitement. Peek-a-boo is not just an aimless activity, it is a brain grower. So forget chess and suduko, just jump out at someone from behind a door, you'll be doing them a big favour, upping their IQ by thousands.

The memory of how Mommy is with Baby influences the baby's physiology, biology, neurology and psychology. How the brain grows is affected by how she put you down, held, smiled, ignored or forgot you; she is the uber-regulator, the big boss of brain development. The neural clusters for social and emotional learning are sculpted by Mommy's attunement with Baby. She grows these neurons in the baby by making direct eye contact with her left eye to Baby's right eye. This is why Mommies usually hold babies in their left arm so this eye contact is made easier. When they gaze into each others' eyes, their hearts, brains and minds are linking up. These face-to-face interactions increase oxygen consumption and energy. Also holding the baby in this position means it can hear Mommy's heartbeat. Seeing her loving face looking down on Baby triggers high levels of endogenous opiates so he experiences pleasure in later social interactions by the positive and exciting stimulation from Mommy.

If the mother is too connected, this affects Baby and later he might feel people are encroaching on his space. If, on the other hand, she is too disconnected, he might in later life feel abandoned and become a comedian looking for constant attention. If the mother soothes the terrified baby, he learns to regulate his own fear. The mother's face shows him what is safe and what isn't. If she shows fear or any negative state, the baby internalizes it. If she expresses depression or shows an expressionless face, the baby, not being able to think something is wrong with the mother, believes he is the cause and so has a greater chance of having depression or some other mental dysfunction himself, while keeping an idealized image of his caretaker; his survival depends on her. Babies are built to engage and respond to the world. If they don't get a response, they stop engaging with the world and can become emotionally frozen.

The holding and separating which are repeated by mother and child, help baby to self-regulate throughout his life while he learns how to care for himself. When the mother over-holds you can soon see the results; every Jewish boy's first novel is about mothers who never let go.

Neuroplasticity

As I said right at the beginning of this book, it was thought about ten years ago that, gene-wise, you're hard-wired from birth; imprisoned by your DNA. But now science has broken that shackle; change is possible well into old age. It was thanks to a scientist named Michael Meaney that the idea of genetic determinism was toppled like the Berlin Wall; here one day, gone the next. His experiments on rats showed that the way a mother treats her babies determines which genes in the offspring's brains are turned on and which are turned off, demonstrating that the genes we're born with are simply nature's opening shot. The genes that make you shy, resilient, anxious, exuberant are shaped by maternal behaviour. If maternal behaviour changes, the genes change. Fearful baby rats were put with nurturing mother rats and were licked rather than ignored and their actual genetic expression changed, proving we're not held captive by our genes.

(I wouldn't have wanted my mother to lick me but perhaps it would have made me more positive and loving. Who am I to say?) But the point is, as I lead you into Part 4, just to remind you that the brain changes continuously by every sight, sound, taste, touch, thought, feeling etc. Experience and learning remodel new circuits (neurogenesis).

We do know some of our ingredients and what they do and maybe in years to come we'll be able to carry around some kind of recipe where we can change who we are day by day. We might decide we want to take a tablespoon of oxytocin and dribble in some dopamine to make us feel good about finishing our homework.

But for right now, the practice of mindfulness gives you some of the utensils that help you turn something you burnt and destroyed into something that tastes good and feels soothing inside.

One Last Thing

Before I move onto Part 4, I just want to bring your attention to how misguided we are in insisting the external world is exactly as we see it. Much of what you see out there is manufactured by your brain, painted in like computer-generated graphics in a movie; only a very small part of the inputs to your occipital lobe comes directly from the external world, the rest comes from internal memory stores and other processes. Think of the area in your visual cortex, a projection room creating what's out there from incoming information. In actuality we see the world in single snapshots and it is a part of your brain makes it seem like it's constantly moving. There are about 70 separate areas working to create a cohesive picture of the world; one part contributes colour, another movement, another edges, another picks up shapes and another shadows. There is no single part that gets the whole picture. And in completely different zones, the images get a name, or an association or an emotional tag.

Sorry to be the bearer of bad news again; we live in a *virtual reality*. Think of *The Wizard of Oz* – you're being run by the guy behind the curtain. You get clips that randomly come into your consciousness never the whole film. So while you're getting these fleeting clips to make you feel that's all that's going on, a trillion things without you knowing it are going on right now inside of you.

When you wake up in the morning, you remember who you were the day before because of billions of neurons, electrically zapping around the brain, working around the clock to make you believe you have unity and keep you wanting to exist.

Another thing your remarkable brain is doing is keeping your heart beating more than 100,000 times per day, that's 40 million heartbeats per year, pumping two gallons of blood per minute, through a system of vascular channels about 60,000 miles in length or twice the circumference of the Earth. Should I go on? (Skip the rest of this if it gets too much.) Just now 100,000 chemical reactions took place in every single one of your cells. Multiply 100,000 chemical reactions by the 70 to 100 trillion cells that make up you. (I couldn't do that but maybe you can.) So while your bodies doing its 'thing' you could be using your mind to bring you calm and happiness. What a segue to introduce you to mindfulness.

Part Four

Mindfulness – Taming Your Mind

My Story

This study of neuroscience gave me reassurance
through discovering that under our scalps, if you
peel us back, we all look pretty much the same.
Knowing this I felt I was part of the human race.
What a relief. (Good news for me, bad news for the
human race). But the course at Oxford was not just
about the brain, it was about learning mindfulness. I
thought in my case, what with the Wagnerian
opera playing 24/7, I'd never be able to find the
inner peace as advertized on the label. For a start,
how would I sit still when I was a professional
hunter of blue-striped cushions? I only decided to
go along with it because I discovered that there's
just one letter separating medication with meditation so I figured, why not? (I had to go to Oxford
for this?)

I probably don't need to mention that I was very,
very sceptical about learning something connected
to meditation. I thought it was a Buddhist thing
where you have to use those words; like shuranana
murtisugamutisatimanyannanaan, an explosion of
meaningless letters. Also, I was not about to
worship some elephant with a thousand arms or a
smiling fat man. Before I become involved, I always
want things to be tangible; things I can see or taste
or touch. Also if someone ever waves a crystal at
me, or tries to read my aura, I politely continue the
conversation, smiling and nodding my head in
agreement; inside they are dead for me. I might

even take their phone number but ultimately I will throw it away.

With mindfulness the rumour is wrong that the point is to empty your mind; you need your mind to analyze, memorize, create and most importantly exist. It can never be empty while you're alive, even in a coma your mind is still chattering away. The trick is to learn to live with the unrelenting sound track.

It isn't easy. Mindfulness is like training in a mental boot camp, it is not for the fainthearted because the mind is like a wild animal demanding you obey its every whim. And you've become so used to being the slave, you obey, 'Gotta do this, gotta write email, gotta garden, gotta learn judo, gotta row across the Atlantic.' The 'gottas' never stop and we always do as we are told. It's so much easier to go along with what you're used to; certainty is less threatening than uncertainty even if you suffer because of it. Most of us believe that fundamentally we can't change and that our thoughts define who we are. This is why you hear the expression, 'It's beyond my control.' People think that their thoughts are fixed and unchangeable.

Taming Your Mind

With mindfulness practice, you eventually tame, calm and befriend that bucking bronco of a mind, gently taking the reins and steering it where you want. If you whip or treat a horse cruelly it will most likely throw you into the dirt and probably stamp on you for luck. If you're gentle with it, soothing it, giving it a little stroke, a shard of straw and lovingly shout 'whoa', it will eventually calm down. Same with the mind; if you're self-critical and demanding, not only do you suffer but now you admonish yourself for your suffering with, 'Why do I feel this way? I shouldn't feel this way. I'm making myself feel this way because I'm such a . . . (fill in the blank but make it nasty).' When the mind gets agitated and negative, if you are patient and gentle with yourself, it eventually settles down and you experience something we call peace and, at best, happiness. (For those of us who have been the biggest bullies to ourselves for most of our lives this is a big challenge.)

It's similar to when you have an argument with someone, if you keep up the aggression, the conflict continues; if one person begins to show empathy and kindness, it dies down from a gale force to a gust of wind.

This does not mean you sit there like a lump of tofu with a bindi on your head, listening to the sitar; it means when your mind does what all of our minds do, which is change – change constantly and never stop chattering – you don't fight it but rather understand and accept it for what it is.

When you stand back and just watch your thoughts and feelings, you find yourself less scattered, more anchored and clearer thinking. Negative thoughts aren't bad in themselves but when we ruminate we're giving ourselves a double whammy. I'm thinking, 'I'm a failure, therefore I must be a failure to think this way'. When you feel you're knee-deep in a negative mood, it's not only the mood that causes the ultimate suffering; it's how you react to it. So not only did an arrow shoot you, which hurts, you send in another one to punish yourself for hurting. That second arrow you shoot at yourself for feeling anxious, stressed or depressed is by far the most agonizing. Pain exists but suffering is optional. You can't stop the unhappy mood but you can stop what happens next. Fear is in fact never as bad as the fear of fear.

We don't survive without emotions and thoughts, they are signals to get our needs met, otherwise mama don't eat or get new shoes. These emotions have evolved to help us do something about sticky situations we find ourselves in; fear is triggered by danger lurking, sadness is evoked when something of value is lost. Disgust is felt when something is rotten. Anger arises when a goal is blocked. All of these feelings are temporary, they are there to alert you in order for you to remedy the problem, quick. When the situation is resolved, the high octane of any of these emotions defuses. The only reason emotions stick around is because of our own emotional reactions to them. The problem isn't the fear or the sadness; it's how our minds react to those feelings. When we try to get rid of the feelings, we create tension, which makes the situation much worse.

Sometimes, I get this familiar ache in my heart and a sense of stabbing emptiness around my ribcage. I don't even know what brings it on; it's just familiar like a horrible visitor. What brings me to my knees though, is the even bigger heart-hurt when I recognize this ghastly guest is back again.

My Story

Perhaps it was my depression that made it an emergency to practise mindfulness. It's not because I'm holier than thou, it's because I seriously needed some way to distinguish my negative but helpful voices from the ones only Satan could have recorded. The problem with depression is you don't see it coming. Routinely practising mindfulness gives me the ability to keep my ear to the ground to pick up early warnings; the pitter-patter of the Earth vibrating before a tsunami. I'm sure it's the same for those with physical disabilities; they have no choice but to do daily exercises for pain control. The routine practices of mindfulness and physical exercise are the most effective ways to a better life but most of us would do anything to avoid them. This seems to be universal in the human condition; we avoid what's good for us, don't ask me why.

Mindfulness means intentionally paying attention, in the present moment, in a non-judgmental way (you don't snap at yourself when you notice you might not be in a good place). Once you stand back, you don't try to make things different, it's not even about relaxation but about witnessing whatever's going on without the usual critical commentary. Rather than run away or repress negative thoughts and feelings, you learn to relate to them from a different angle, experience them through a different lens. It's the effort of trying to change things from what they are that ultimately exhausts us.

Mindfulness is not complicated, it's what we can all do: notice things. Just by standing back and being aware, it immediately gives you a new view of your inner and outer world along with internal changes in the brain (discussed later). By sharpening your focus on what's happening right now, you start to notice that thoughts aren't facts, they're constantly changing patterns; they come and go, transform, disperse and dissolve. Finally you can experience them, not as something solid or threatening but as ambient background noise. The idea is to relate to thoughts as merely brain events, rather than absolute truths. Thoughts are not who you are, they're habitual patterns in the mind, nothing more and as soon as you see them that way, they lose their sting. I think of them as the noise of a radio in another room; I can pay attention, sing along with them if I want and also choose to ignore them. The big idea is: THOUGHTS ARE NOT YOUR MASTER, THEY ARE YOUR SERVANT.

That Old Mind Keeps on Rolling Along

The mind is always collecting and collating information from the senses, the environment or other parts of the mind. Regulating the mind is like driving a car and constantly having to shift gears to adjust to ever-changing road conditions. As each gear has a purpose so have these shifts in the mind. The car can be on automatic or on manual, same with the mind; you can choose to respond automatically or you can choose to override it. It's impossible for a car to be in two gears at once. Same with the mind; it can't be in two modes at once because they both require the same mental machinery.

Mindfulness teaches you to be aware of what mental gear you're in and gives you the skills to disengage and engage when you choose. The two modes of mind, automatic and manual, could be called 'doing' and 'being' modes. The practice of mindfulness sharpens your focus so you can do something about your mind being constantly distracted and mentally hi-jacked. You can do something about those voices, hurrah!

'Doing' Mode

We live in a constant state of wanting and this need for success is embedded in our culture. If we don't reach these self-imposed goals, we may experience a sense of worthlessness. In my opinion this is why so many people over-shop. They might feel they have no worth but their clothes do.

Here is another great gift/glitch: our ability to fill the gap between wanting something and figuring out how to get it. That's what makes us a superior species, the fact that we can review past events in order to ensure successful outcomes in the future; filling that gap between where we are and where we want to be is probably our biggest motivational driver. That's how a star is born. This is how we achieve, create, produce and hit the deadline; if we didn't have this ability we would still be sea slugs. There is a fine line between actually wanting to accomplish something and just hard-core desire and that's where the rips and tears of the human fabric might start. When we get something we want badly, the wanting diminishes, which is great news until the next want comes along. This puts us into a constant state (see dopamine) of want, need, lust, greed and most of the seven deadly sins. (Please don't let me tarnish your trophies for those of you who have just won an academy award or a medal in the Olympics – well done, really.)

Another tear in the psyche happens when this need to fill the gap switches on and suddenly we want to know things like, 'Why aren't I taller, sexier, more successful?' The trouble is the mind can't distinguish between cognitive problem-solving and those rhetorical questions, 'Why did he dump me? Why don't I get more tweets? I should be happier, more successful, prettier . . .' Each of these questions only leads to another and another and because there is no ultimate answer, you'll fall back to your old leitmotif: 'I can't find a solution so I must be a failure/weak/stupid.' (Pick your poison.)

These gaps in knowledge are impossible to fill because there are no answers to the above and they can only lead to more questions, this is why so many existentialists went crazy from thinking too much about, 'Why do we suffer?' That cannot be answered, even if you're Sartre and smoke in Parisian cafés with your smirky, beardy friends. All those, 'if only' or 'I should have' concepts end in tears. This is why some of us are dragged through our lives chasing status, goals and approval (see stand up comedians). That's the glitch in our machinery, we have to fill that gap to find a solution and so we go into a frenzy of analyzing until we come up with nothing, then we head into the hills of 'What's wrong with me, I must be an idiot'. Sulking is the problem not the solution. And the mind will be in such a frenzy of analyzing the past or future that the present is of no use at all on the problem-solving front.

Critical thinking is one of our highest achievements besides eating with a fork, so when we emotionally can't get what we want, we have to think our way towards the resolution and this where we crash and burn.

My Story

I don't know if I need to mention my permanent residence at the 'doing-mode hotel'. My daily routine, before I started mindfulness, involved jolting up from bed at six in the morning after terrifying nightmares of things I forget to do, followed by a seizure of panic about having to buy a snorkel, which I wouldn't need until my next holiday, six months away. But I felt it would be life-threatening if I didn't hunt one down in five minutes. Like the guy in *Dr Strangelove*, my arm would automatically fling out to grab my computer to Google 'snorkel' but at the same time I had to check my emails with the same urgency as Obama probably has when checking if North Korea has detonated any nuclear bombs. You can imagine this 'doing' mode lead to my demise.

Just a note: this obsessive quality to get things done 'now' at the speed of light has given me success. The problem as always is, I couldn't find the 'off' switch so everything was done at this pace consistently leading to burnout. This is a warning to all alphas, whether they're male or female.

The lesson is: how you make money can either make you sick or successful – or both. It's up to you. As long as you're aware you are in 'doing' mode, it won't take over your life. Mindfulness means making a mental note of the state you're in, no matter what that state is. It's about noticing,

> 'Oh, my mind is really a mess with thousands of red hot messages soaring around in there.' And not with the accompanying, 'I did this to myself, I'm a screw-up.' Or worse depending on how punishing you are to yourself.

Automatic Pilot

Another kick in the ass/gift from evolution is our ability to go on automatic pilot. We need it so as not to have to think about every detail it takes to navigate our environment, so we clump all the minuscule movements together and do things without having to think about them. This is to conserve energy in our brain so each time we learn an activity, we don't have to think step-by-step; we don't have to think, 'put key in, turn on engine, look in rear view mirror, release brake' or 'reach out for fork, bring to mouth, chew, swallow, etc . . .' Our brains can daisy-chain thousands of actions together and make them feel seamless; the information goes into our unconscious and we can be asleep at the wheel.

You can do almost anything in your life on automatic pilot; the problem is you'll miss most of your life just going from one automatic activity to the next and it becomes habit-forming. You could end up thinking, eating, reading, getting married and dying in a haze of unawareness. Some people do. What happens is that you live on autopilot and miss noticing what's happening before your very eyes, paying no attention to the present moment. If you're continually on automatic pilot, you won't know that your life has turned into a to-do list. Later down the line, even seeing a friend becomes yet another chore.

Mindfulness – Taming Your Mind

Some handy questions to find out how much time you spend on autopilot:

A. When you sit down to eat do you find yourself an hour later having no idea what you just put in your mouth?

B. Do you throw a party and then wake up the next morning with no idea what happened and you don't drink?

C. Ever get in your car and then have no memory of how you got where you were going, probably leaving a trail of dead people?

D. Ever come back from a holiday and need photos to remember anything?

E. Ever look in the mirror and think 'where have I been for the last 20 years?'

F. Ever leave your house and realize you forgot to put on your underpants?

There are no correct answers to these questions because they happen to all of us. Except Oprah and the Dalai Lama.

Depressing Thought

Here's a depressing thought. Suppose your life expectancy is 90 and you're 38 now, that means you have approximately 52 years left. Now let's say you're only aware of a minute every three to five days, this might mean you only have about 12 years left in conscious time. I may not have this exactly right but you see my point? (I hardly do) but what I'm trying to say is that if you were attentive to your life rather than simply getting through it, then even if a doctor told you you only had six months to live, if you were awake to every minute, it would be longer than if you had 100 years to live in an unconscious state. Billions of dollars are spent on longevity. If we lived more mindfully, relishing each moment, think of the saving. We could toss away those vitamins, moisturizers and surgical appliances because it would seem as if we were living forever. (I point the finger at me on the surgical front.)

'Being' Mode

Some people may think, 'Oh, God what happens if I get stuck in the 'being' mode and I just end up like a houseplant?' Worry not; our default state of mind is that 'go get it' state (otherwise no one would ever endeavour to fly first class.)

The 'doing' mode gives you the 'go get' to fill the gap between wanting and getting, while the 'being' mode has no voice, it's just directly sensing something; and being in the eye of the experience. It's not about 'spacing out' or 'chilling' (no idea what it means, other than getting cosy with my ice cubes) but I experience it when I'm scuba diving; being completely present in a state of bliss and at one with the fish.

Everyone has felt something like this at some point; looking at a sunset, stroking your cat, smiling at a seagull, a moment where time stops and you are not so consumed with 'you'. In this mode, the mind isn't flipping between the past and the future, it has nothing to do, nowhere to go, so it can start to settle and slow down from the high-speed chaos, noticing what's going on in front of your eyes at that moment and experiencing thoughts as passing phenomena that arise and disappear. This state of 'being', as hippy as it sounds, is something that is actually natural to us. It's whenever you experience something directly without added running commentary. You can still accomplish things but you do them without the over-bearing, over-burning drive. As Lady Macbeth says, 'Thou art not without ambition, but without the illness should attend it.' (She knew a thing or two about mental health.)

'Doing'/'Being' – Working Together

With mindfulness, you learn to distinguish these two states, shifting mental gears and deciding when you want to be in one or the other – remember, it's like the gears of a car, you cannot be in both manual and automatic at the same time. There may be times you want to let your mind wander (great ideas come out of daydreaming) reminisce about the past or make plans for the future but when you want to pay attention you can switch your focus like the beam of a search light. You'll learn through practise to distinguish when one state is useful and when it isn't. You might be happily regurgitating some old images and suddenly hours or days have passed without you realizing you've been locked in and chained down in memory lane. You could go through a whole lifetime in your head dreaming of another life, instead of living your own.

Steve Jobs, chief executive of Apple and a meditator said, 'Remembering that I'll be dead soon is the most important tool I've ever encountered to help me make the big choices in life because almost everything – all external expectations, all pride, all fear of embarrassment or failure – all these things just fall away in the face of death, leaving only what is truly important.'

My Story

When my kids were growing up I could rarely slow down, I was in that full driven 'doing' mode most of the time. I remember one of my kids once trying to get my attention to show me his dead hamster and help him deal with the funeral arrangements. I couldn't pull the phone away I was so consumed with whatever I was shouting about. I tried to pretend I was interested in the hamster situation but I couldn't take that receiver away from my ear. My kids told me they thought I had two phones growing out of each side of my head like earmuffs. Even one Christmas, when I was dressed as Santa, I hid a speaker in my beard; they knew it and have never stopped busting me about it to this day. They keep asking me what were they like at certain ages and how they acted; I have to check videos to come back with an answer. I'm ashamed to say my

> mind was elsewhere, either thinking or worrying
> about the work I didn't get or work I did get. I wish
> I had practised mindfulness when my kids were
> small; I'd be able to remember the dead hamster's
> name.

Learning About Mindfulness

If you want to learn mindfulness, you go to a mindfulness-trained instructor to do an eight-week course, two hours a session. For me the instruction manual *is* learning these skills but please don't think I'm a fanatic and this is the only way to see the light. Everyone will have their own way of 'taming' their mind. But whatever you choose to do, it has to be something that doesn't involve running away, encouraging denial, repression or simply drugging yourself to hide from your own thoughts and feelings. It has to teach you to manage your mind; that way happiness lies. If you can focus your attention at will from the driven mind to the present mind, put down this book; you are probably evolved and have no reason to read on. But if you find that, rather than face the noise in your mind, you would do almost anything for distraction – obsessively clean the house, phone everyone you know and even don't know, email the world, get stoned too often, hit the to-do list – keep reading.

The Development of Mindfulness

It all began with Dr Jon Kabat-Zinn, who set up the Stress Reduction Clinic at the University of Massachusetts Medical

School. Since then, he and his team have helped more than 10,000 people with a range of conditions: heart disease, cancer, AIDS, chronic pain, headaches, high blood pressure, sleep disorders, anxiety, panic, gastrointestinal problems and depression. Kabat-Zinn is not a guru in a bedsheet. He is a Professor of Medicine Emeritus and received his PhD in molecular biology from M.I.T. He created a method to use on patients whose pain was too chronic to remedy; those that were given the final diagnosis of 'You're going to have to live with this'.

He came up with a method called 'mindfulness-based stress reduction,' teaching his patients that, by focusing in on their painful sensations rather than distracting themselves, they'd eventually relate differently and notice that pain was not something solid but a continuously changing landscape. By becoming aware of how transitory it is, the pain would eventually lose its vicelike grip. He found that if you try and ignore the pain, you're probably tensing other parts of the body, therefore creating stress somewhere else.

Physical Pain

So much of pain is reacting to it, wanting it to go away, hating it and cursing yourself for having it, but if you explore the bare sensations by going right into it you'll notice that the sensations lose their solidity. Pain is the pure physical 'ouch' and suffering is the story you give yourself about that 'ouch'. If it becomes unbearable, try to shift your attention to an area where you don't feel pain and let your mind rest there. This isn't about nailing yourself to a cross. This is about choosing where to focus your attention.

EXERCISE FOR PHYSICAL PAIN

You can feel this for yourself, even if you don't suffer from chronic pain, by stretching or bending a part of your body to the point of discomfort, but without stretching beyond your limits. If you send your attention right into that specific region of pain, not thinking about it but trying to experience the specific sensations – whether they're burning, throbbing, stabbing or pulsing – you'll notice that pain isn't solid or constant but rather a series of sensations, sometimes hard, sometimes light and even sometimes gone altogether. Go on, try it – flex or bend any part of your body to the point where is starts to ache, and see if you can send your focus directly into that region. Remember to be kind to yourself.

My Story

When I was having a root canal recently, I tried to deal with the pain by shifting my attention to an area where I wasn't in complete agony. I tried to send my attention to my toenails. That didn't work so I tried to picture myself in the Bahamas. That didn't work either so I attempted to sing to myself to calm myself down. That didn't work either but I started to see how hilarious it was; me with my mouth wide open singing lullabies to myself accompanied by the drill. I still had the pain but it took a backseat.

MBCT

Mark Williams (my professor), John Teasdale and Zindel Segal all worked together to apply Kabat-Zinn's theories to emotional pain and called it 'mindfulness-based cognitive therapy' (MBCT). They began their work with those suffering from depression and taught patients, just like with physical pain, not to try and suppress it but to see if they could locate exactly where the sensation of the emotion is in the body. When you focus in, very gently, on the exact location of where you feel anger, fear, stress or heartbreak, you'll notice those sensations lose their intensity; they're always coming and going, getting deeper and lighter. They're always changing and change is the only thing in life you can depend on.

EXERCISE – EMOTIONS

Focus in on a predominant feeling and *notice* where an emotion arises in the body and explore (just as with pain) into the core of the feeling, the edges, pulsing, throbbing or stabbing. *Notice* how eager your mind is to create a story out of a feeling. (The story might not even have anything to do with the feeling. The mind always wants an explanation.) Just stick with the feeling, and skip the running commentary.

My Story

This just happened to me today. I was asked to take part in a televised charity event (no names). (Behind the laughing showbiz mask beats a heart of gold.) Everyone who's anyone in the entertainment world wants this job. Well, this year I wasn't asked to go to the fly-ridden country, I wasn't asked to go anywhere. I was asked to go on radio and introduce raising money by playing a prank on David Cameron. So I'm in mid-radio plug, when I'm handed notes about how the prank will raise funds and I see I am not the presenter of this event, someone else is. I am there merely to promote the event.

My stomach dropped 30,000 feet even though I never left the building, as my ego was shot down in flames. Being a professional, I carried on without a flicker of bitterness showing. The interviewer actually asked what I had to do with the event and I smiled graciously and said, 'Nothing'. Ok, here's the point, I'm there to talk about a charity that prevents starvation and fights disease and I'm caught in a narcissistic, egotistical massacre. Believe me, I am the first to be aware of how despicable my thoughts are, the thoughts of shame and self-loathing bombarding my brain.

It's at moments like this that you really don't want to feel the full brunt of being carpet-bombed by your own thoughts but here's the bitch; no matter how much you want to try to run from these recriminating thoughts, they're there bubbling away under the surface.

No matter how many decathlons you run, how many shoes you buy or how famous you get, those unresolved, unbearable feelings exist below. Freud was on the button when he said you have to bring your darkness into the light if you want to free yourself from those deep unconscious emotions. Just like a virus has to be sweated out, your malignant thoughts and feelings have to surface.

EXERCISE – R.A.I.N.

You could use the acronym R.A.I.N. when you're dealing with your emotions. It stands for Recognition, Acceptance, Investigation and Non-identification.

Recognition

Ever feel overwhelmed? You can't think clearly, your head is full of red mist? First, just recognize whatever you can snatch from the melee, such as fear, rage or sadness. Even identifying an emotion means you're regulating it; you're using your prefrontal cortex to calm the inflamed limbic system.

Acceptance

All emotions are Ok, it's how you think about them that does the damage. Whatever the feeling is, it is just a feeling, you don't have to act on it. Let it pass through because in the next second it changes anyway. Dump the shame and blame, it will never get you anywhere but back in your head.

Investigation

You send the focus of attention into wherever the emotional pain is in your body. As soon as you tune into body sensation, the story ends. Go inside: is your chest tightening? Your stomach churning? Your jaw clenched like *The Alien*? If you register nothing , that's fine too.

Non-Identification

This means stepping away from the emotions and giving them space so you get that 'this too shall pass' vibe. With this distancing, you're developing self-regulation, taking the heat off, paradoxically, turning into the bare sensations rather than the 'whys' and 'wherefores'. You won't automatically snap out of your sadness and skip through fields but you'll give yourself that gap to take the burn off and reflect in the midst of it all. The more you practise, the faster you get at identifying and exploring your emotions.

EXERCISE - FIVE SECONDS (STOP AND NOTICE)

Suggestions:

Set the phone to 'ting' every few hours and when it 'tings', *stop and notice* what's going on in your mind and body and then move on – simple.

When you close your computer, *stop and notice* what's going on in your mind and body and then move on.

When you finish or start eating, *stop and notice* what's going on in your mind and body and then move on.

Here are some daily activities you can use for the five second exercise.

Options
Brushing your teeth
Taking a shower
Washing the dishes
Taking out the garbage
Doing the laundry
Opening your computer
Peeling carrots (my idea of hell)
Seeing your kids

Got the idea?

BONUS SUGGESTION – Use the five-second pause when you *notice* yourself going into the 'doing' mode, i.e. when you get the first hint that you're starting to mindlessly go from one activity to the next to the next; before you find yourself in the 'endless list' syndrome.

EXERCISE - S.T.O.P.

You notice your mind is wandering, ruminating or not where you want it to be. Don't! Don't! Don't punish yourself! Just S.T.O.P.

S – STOP whatever you're doing to notice what's going on in your mind and body. Whatever's happening up there, don't do anything about it. Just STOP.

T – Stands for THINK. If you are reading this book, THINK, were you actually reading? (I won't get mad if you weren't, this is just an exercise.) If you find that you actually weren't reading, what were you thinking?

EXAMPLES – 'I need tea, coffee, whipped cream, sex, the phone, to send an email, I should have . . . [fill in], I forgot to . . . [fill in], I didn't . . . [fill in].'

Were you in the past, future, planning, worrying, day-dreaming, having erotic thoughts? (That would be weird.)

If you don't know where your mind was, that's Ok. Just register a blank.

The fact that you noticed that your mind was not reading is a great accomplishment. You should blow up the balloons, pop the poppers and congratulate yourself.

If you have been reading all this time and have been aware of not just the words but the sounds around you, the sensation of your breathing and the feel of your body touching whatever you're sitting on, you are an enlightened being. Read on no more, put down this book and call the Dalai Lama. You are next in line.

O – Stands for OPTIONS. If you find your mind is somewhere else, put the book down, close your eyes and pick one of your senses. Focus on:

The sounds around you
The smells around you
The feeling of your body on the chair/bed/sofa whatever you're on
The feeling of your breath going in and out of your nose/throat/chest/abdomen or all the way in and all the way out

P – Is for PROCEED. Go back to reading my book and don't let me find you losing concentration again.

For me this poem by Portia Nelson sums up the benefit of practising mindfulness.

Autobiography in Five Short Chapters

Chapter 1
I walk down the street.
There is a deep hole in the sidewalk.
I fall in.
I am lost . . . I am hopeless.
It isn't my fault.
It takes forever to find a way out.

Chapter 2
I walk down the same street.
There is a deep hole in the sidewalk.
I pretend I don't see it.
I fall in again.
I can't believe I'm in the same place.
But it isn't my fault.
It still takes a long time to get out.

Chapter 3
I walk down the same street.
There is a deep hole in the sidewalk.
I see it is there.
I still fall in . . . it's a habit.
My eyes are open.
I know where I am.
It is my fault.
I get out immediately.

Chapter 4
I walk down the same street.
There is a deep hole in the sidewalk.
I walk around it.

Chapter 5
I walk down another street.

Anchoring

You might find that just to 'pause' is enough, to relish those few seconds when you come out of your busy-ness and are able to 'smell the roses' or bathe in what it feels like to be present before going back to what you need to do.

The practice of MBCT gives you the tools so that you become your own shrink (big money-saver). You learn to observe your own thoughts. But how do you do that without falling into rumination? Because that's how our minds work, always trying to fathom out why we have a problem. With mindfulness you learn a technique of focusing on an anchor, which you can return to when the mind gets too agitated or tries to suck you into its never-ending story. This anchor isn't some wand you have to find in fairyland, it's something we all come equipped with: our senses.

The idea is you focus on one of your senses; listening, seeing, tasting, smelling, touching or breathing, and when your mind wanders, which all minds do, you *notice* where your mind has gone and then, without any criticism, take or escort your focus back to one of the senses. When you give your full attention to any of these, your autopilot switches off, your mind stops ricocheting from past to future because you don't have to think about a sense, you just experience it. If you pay close attention to what you're immediately experiencing, you're right there in the present; the mind-wandering mode switches off. The brain of someone who is totally focused on one point (someone who has practised mindfulness even for a few days) has lowered amygdala activity (fear button is 'off') he also has a steady heartbeat and normal blood pressure. He is in a state of well-being.

These anchors provide a place to go back to when you notice rumination beginning. So if you want to investigate how your mind works by practising mindfulness, you can choose to NOTICE where your mind went and then return to a safe harbour by focusing on a sense or the breath. And by noticing without reprimanding yourself and having a safe base, you'll see thoughts and feelings as mental phenomena that aren't threatening. You're strengthening your ability to tune into your mind when you need to create, make decisions, problem-solve, compare etc. and tune out when your thinking becomes harmful or too critical. What you think about is your choice – you're not the victim of what you think.

What Anchor to Choose?

It's up to you what you want to focus on but when you've made your choice, the idea is to try and attend to it for a specific amount of time, otherwise you've still got a mind that jumps from thought to thought. Some people choose to focus on their breath because it's always there and its pattern changes, so you never get bored, as you follow your inhaling and exhaling.

When I'm onstage and I start to lose it, there follows a chain of reactions: my body seizes up, heart starts pounding, panic rises and I get the old theme tune, 'I'm going to flop. Everyone hates me.' An audience can always feel your fear and for some evolutionary reason turns hostile, howling like animals baying for blood. It must be some primitive instinct that when someone is failing in front of a large group of people, they, as a gaggle, go in for the kill.

From practising mindfulness, I've learnt that to save my skin, as soon as I recognize I'm going into the high-anxiety mode either by a physical signal (dry mouth, beating heart) or an emotional signal (a stabbing in the stomach), I send my attention to my feet, and their contact with the floor. As soon as my focus goes from thoughts to a sensation, the red mist drains from my brain and I can think again. And when I'm calm and in control, the audience gets calm. It doesn't have to be attention to your feet, using any of your senses can be used.

Anchor Options

All of these anchors take the focus from the busy mind to the experience of a sense, which is always immediate. (You can't hear, taste, touch or smell something in the past or future but right now.)

Staying focused without force strengthens the part of the brain that allows you to switch focus when you want to move from the 'doing' mind to the 'being' mind.

You're learning to experience without judgment, treating thoughts and feelings as mental events without identifying with them.

You're learning to be aware of what is there without trying to change or fix things.

By focusing on sight, sound, taste and touch you're learning that everything takes shape and then dissolves.

You're learning to move focus more adeptly from one area to another and also from a narrow focus; the touch of your foot on the ground to a wide focus; a sense of the whole body from head to toe.

Everyone's mind constantly grabs for attention: if you need to do this 100 times then do it 100 times, just like you did the first time. And this is taming your mind.

EXERCISE – FOCUS ON YOUR FEET

Stand or sit on a chair with your feet on the floor, with your spine straight but not rigid; your eyes can be open or shut (I shut mine, if you want to keep your eyes open then simply lower your gaze). Now send your attention to the feel of your feet on the ground. *Notice* the precise sensations, the weight, temperature, tingling or nothing at all. *Notice* when your mind takes over with its commentary and as soon as it does, note where it took you (without judgment) and bring your focus back to your feet. Sounds simple? Try it. How long before your mind grabs you back?

EXERCISE – TASTE

Place a piece of chocolate in your mouth. (Now you can get the percentage of actual cocoa in the chocolate. What were we eating before? Paper?) If chocolate isn't your thing, you can choose anything else, as long as it's something you'd put in your mouth and swallow. (Use discretion please – no weirdos.)

Slowly put it on your tongue. *Notice* when your mind has snatched the attention back and where it's taken you and then gently take your focus back to the chocolate. Feel the weight and texture. Is it sweet? Is it salty? *Notice* the sensation of biting, chewing and swallowing.

Think of your mouth as a laboratory and your tongue your workbench to explore taste. In the past, how many times have you thrown a chocolate in your mouth but your mind was somewhere else? You maybe swooned with the first bite but after a few more chews your mind takes flight to another town. You might even have tasted the first and last bite but were asleep for the bites in between. You paid for the whole chocolate but missed most of the action, not to mention, with the enormous calorie intake, you've fattened up your thighs without any epicurean benefit.

EXERCISE – FOCUS ON YOUR SEAT

Wherever you're sitting and whatever you're sitting on, *notice* the feeling of the back of your thighs, pelvis or whatever is touching the chair. *Notice* when your mind pulls you away, and move your focus back to your seat on the seat.

EXERCISE – LISTENING TO SOUND

Bring your attention to all the sound around you and tune in like it's your favourite record. Pick up sounds in front, behind, above, below and the silences in between the sounds. As soon as you *notice* that your mind wandered, take the focus back to the sound.

EXERCISE – BREATHING

Many people use breathing as a point of focus because it gives you a direct insight into your emotional state; noticing the speed and quality (shallow or harsh) of your breath gives you a way to detect your own internal weather patterns. It makes a great anchor because when you notice your mind has wandered, your breath is always there, you don't have to go hunting for it; the breath is always breathing.

So following your breath, it's best to stay with one area either through your nose, throat, chest or abdomen so your mind stays focused. NOTICE how your breath changes with each inhale and exhale: if it's light, heavy, short or long, just noticing that it's always changing and dissolving.

EXERCISE - SMELLING

Smell a lemon/coffee/bread/a baby's head . . . where you stick your nose is up to you. *Notice* every subtlety of the scent and when your mind takes you away, *notice* where it's gone and come back to the smell.

EXERCISE – TOUCH

You don't need to be in any special place to experience mindfulness, it's just about being awake to sensation. You can simply pet your cat/dog/husband . . . your choice. *Notice* the feel of the fur/hair if your mind takes over, *notice* where it's been and come back to the feeling of petting your pet/husband. (They may be the same thing.)

EXERCISE – THINKING

The problem with thinking is when we confuse the thoughts about things with the things themselves. We can think about an imaginary frog in our minds and know it's not the same as a real frog. But when our minds bring up something that physically doesn't exist, such as our self-esteem, it's hard to see the distinction. Thoughts about our self-esteem are no more real than an imaginary frog. If we switch to the 'being' mode we can see this much more clearly. We can stand back and witness our thoughts and feelings as experiences that come and go in our mind just like sounds, tastes and sights. So when a thought comes up, 'I feel like a failure', we don't have to take it as a reality and fall into the inevitable rumination. (It's just an imaginary frog.)

EXERCISE – EXPERIENCING THINKING ITSELF

Just as with sounds, *notice* your thoughts as events in the mind simply as noise rather than trying to follow the meaning. Some people imagine their thoughts are like clouds in the sky; some are heavy, some light, some threatening but they all keep moving and changing. You can choose whether to jump on one of them but it would be like jumping on a cloud, they aren't solid structures so you'll fall through.

Another metaphor is to imagine your thoughts on a cinema screen and you're watching from the audience. *Notice* when you find yourself in the film, among the characters caught up in the plot. As soon as you've noticed without judgment walk back to your seat and watch the film again. The idea is to watch how you get caught, step back and then re-engage. This is called *untangled perception*.

EXERCISE - MOVING

A very portable way of bringing awareness into your daily life is mindfully walking. (You really can't get more portable than this.) You're not trying to get anywhere you're just noticing each step at a time. *Notice* exactly how you experience your walk, how automatically one foot lifts while the other touches the ground. *Notice* the muscles working inside your legs and what happens to your balance. *Notice* your weight on the ground. *Notice* how you quickly your mind kicks in because we rarely just walk, we're usually moving our thinking minds around and our legs happen to be moving. As soon as you find yourself lost in thought or making judgments on how you move bring the focus back to the movement.

Your body is always with you; it's your most accessible anchor. Just be *in* your body as you move, reach, grab, scratch, run. All you have to do is keep bringing your attention back again and again to your body bringing you right into the moment.

EXERCISE – WIDENING THE FOCUS

You can stay focused on a specific sense in your body, or you can choose to open up your lens of awareness to every sense, all at once, from your head to your toes.

Being Mindful with Stress

Our reactions to stress are automatic and we are loaded up to the brim with it, from simply getting a plumber to worrying about some ice cap out there somewhere defrosting. Because most of our lives now, thanks to our ever-speedier culture, are lived in a state of hyper-arousal, almost everything out there seems scary. We're in a constant downpour of adrenaline and cortisol, muscle tension, high blood pressure and lack of oxygen to the brain; all of which can make us very, very ill.

EXERCISE – STRESS

Notice when you feel the beginning of stress, closely explore where it is in your body; the size, the edges, the sensations. *Notice* how your breathing and your posture change. *Notice* if your mind starts to kick in with suggestions to get coffee, cigarettes, or tranquilizers. You don't have to suppress the thoughts or the feelings of fear, anger or hurt but recognize that they are the dandruff of a flakey mind.

Each time you bring in awareness without trying to change anything, you'll start to see those things that 'pushed your buttons' in the past as familiar themes and start to treat them like old friends you don't really like but have learnt to put up with. I have a girlfriend who never shuts up, with a voice like a buzz saw. I have learnt to love her, even though I can only stand her for ten minutes at a time.

Only with the regular exercise of bringing awareness to negative thoughts and feelings will you be able to break those mental and physical habits. If you learn to ground yourself in your body, your breath or in one of your senses, you'll dampen the anxiety, fear or depression as it's coming down the pipeline so that you can re-balance more quickly. You have lots of opportunities to practise on your stress and you'll fail many times but just by altering your attention, you're creating new patterns of behaviour. Each time we face our feelings head-on rather than run, we're building muscle just like any sportsman when practising his skills.

Acceptance isn't resignation. You don't just lie back in your sombrero saying mañana. It provides you with a means of responding skillfully rather than the usual knee-jerk reaction.

The great thing about all these exercises is they're portable so you can use them anywhere, anytime, in any position. Also it's cheap, in fact it's free.

Last But Not Least - Kindness

When you turn your attention in and listen to your own personal dictator, chances are you'll punish yourself. Knowing that the enemy is not without but within is enough to make you self-flagellate for years. The harder you are on yourself, the louder the critical voice gets. Judging and evaluating are cousins to rumination and the 'doing' mode. When we make any sort of judgment we're comparing how we want things to be, to how they are, and trying to fill that gap. The habit of judging ourselves is what pounds us into the ground.

You're being kind to yourself by intentionally moving your attention from the mind to the body. Your body can withstand emotions; your mind can't because it is hardwired to come up with a solution when there isn't one. Think of the body as a safe harbour when you're being ravaged by the 'Slings and arrows of outrageous fortune'. This is spoken by Hamlet; a man who could have used a class in mindfulness. He went nuts from over-pondering.

If a friend was being abused you wouldn't shout at her to stop suffering, you would soothe her pain. So when you're possessed by the demons of your own making, you should treat yourself like you would that friend. The main thing that calms your mind is compassion for yourself. I know that idea makes many people wince (it does have the whiff of patchouli oil), thinking they're being self-indulgent, but being kind to yourself when you notice your mind has wandered calms down the vicious thought patterns, which in turn impacts the re-wiring of neurons.

Another poem that sums up my experience with mindfulness is this one by Rumi:

The Guest House

This being human is a guest house.
Every morning a new arrival.
A joy, a depression, a meanness,
some momentary awareness comes
as an unexpected visitor.

Welcome and entertain them all!
Even if they're a crowd of sorrows,
who violently sweep your house
empty of its furniture.

Still, treat each guest honorably.
He may be cleaning you out
for some new delight.

The dark thought, the shame, the malice.
Meet them at the door laughing,
and invite them in.

Be grateful for whoever comes,
because each has been sent
as a guide from beyond.

Kindness to Others

Not only is compassion good for our health, but the impact of the hormones we produce in ourselves pass from person to person. We can pass our neuroses but we can also pass our feelings of warmth and kindness. You get a sudden rush of oxytocin which makes you feel safe and soothed and therefore switches it on in others around you. We are social animals, not made for isolation, so all our feelings ripple out to the next person; working like *neural wi-fi* (the emotional pass the parcel). When you're calm and at ease you have the free space in your head to listen to someone else; be curious about his life so that he feels he matters. When you get into the habit of passing warmth, humour and compassion, I'd say you might just experience what happiness feels like. (To me, it feels like someone is tickling my heart.) If you pass on these qualities and the other person lights up with happiness, it comes right back at you.

Facts About Mindfulness

The real reason I began to practise mindfulness seriously was because of the empirical evidence of what happens in the brain. It wasn't good enough that mindfulness helped me deal with the depression or that it brought me calm in the storm, ever the sceptic, I demanded hard-core proof. It appeared I didn't trust my own feelings as much as I did science. There is so much data to show the practice doesn't just ameliorate physical and emotional pain, it sharpens your concentration and focus and therefore gives you the edge when others are floundering in the mud. (If that's what you're after.)

Here is just some of the evidence that swung the jury in favour of mindfulness (for me):

Connection to Feelings
A number of studies have found mindfulness results in increased blood flow to the insula and an increased volume and density of grey matter. This is a crucial area that gives the ability to focus into your body, and connects you to your feelings, such as butterflies in your stomach, or a blow to the heart. Strengthening your insula enhances introspection, which is the key to mindfulness.

Self Control
Researchers found that increased blood flow to the anterior cingulate cortex after just *six 30-minute meditation sessions* strengthened connections to this area, which is crucial for controlling impulse, and may help explain why

mindfulness is effective in helping with self control, i.e. addictions.

Counteracting High Anxiety
Researchers from Stanford found that after an eight-week mindfulness course participants had less reactivity in their amygdala and reported feeling fewer negative emotions.

Quietening the Mind
The brain stem produces neurotransmitters which regulate attention, mood and sleep. These changes may explain why meditators perform better on tests of attention, are less likely to suffer from anxiety and depression and often have improved sleep patterns.

Regulating Emotions
The hippocampus is involved in learning and memory and can help with reactivity to stress. Increased density of neurons in this area may help explain why meditators are more emotionally stable and less anxious.

Regulating Thoughts
Changes in the cerebellum are likely to contribute to meditators' increased ability to respond to life events in a positive way.

Curbing Addictive Behaviour
The prefrontal cortex is involved with self-regulation and decision-making. Mindfulness has been found to increase blood flow to this area, which enhances self-awareness and self-control helping you to make constructive choices and let go of harmful ones.

Curbing OCD

PET scans were performed on 18 OCD patients before and after 10 weeks of mindfulness practice, none took medication and all had moderate to severe symptoms. PET scans after treatment showed activity in the orbital frontal cortex had fallen dramatically meaning the worry circuit was unwired. It was the first study to show that mindfulness-based cognitive therapy has the power to systematically change brain chemistry in a well-identified brain circuit. So, intentionally making a mindful effort can alter brain function and this induces neuroplasticity. This is the first time it was established that mindfulness is a form of experience that promotes neuroplasticity.

A Quicker Brain

Researchers from UCLA have found that meditators have stronger connections between different areas in the brain. This greater connectivity is not limited to specific regions but found across the brain at large. It also increases the ability to rapidly relay information from one area to the next giving you a quicker and more agile brain.

Training Your Brain (As Well As Your Body)

A trained mind is physically different from an untrained mind. You can retain inner strength even though the world around you is frantic and chaotic. People are trying to find the antidotes to suffering so it's time we started doing the obvious; training our brains as we do our bodies. Changing the way you think changes the chemicals in your brain. For example, the less you workout, the lower the level of acetylcholine and the less you have of this chemical, the poorer your ability to pay attention. Even with age-related losses, almost every physical aspect of the brain can recover and new neurons can bloom.

More Positive Research on Mindfulness

- Research from Harvard University suggests that we spend nearly 50% of our day mind-wandering, typically lost in negative thoughts about what might happen, or has already happened to us. There is a mind-wandering network in the brain, which generates thoughts centred around 'me' and is focused in an area called the medial prefrontal cortex. Research has shown that when we practise mindfulness, activity in this 'me' centre decreases. Furthermore, it has been shown that when experienced practitioners' minds do wander, monitoring areas (such as the lateral prefrontal cortex) become active to keep an eye on where the mind is going and if necessary bring attention back to the present, which results in less worrying and more living.

- Researchers from the University of Montreal investigated the differences in how meditators and non-meditators experience pain and how this relates to brain structure. They found that the more experienced the meditators were, the thicker their anterior cingulate cortex and the lower their sensitivity to pain.

- Researchers from Emory University found that the decline in cognitive abilities that typically occurs as we age, such as slower reaction times and speed of thinking, was not found in elderly meditators. Using fMRI, they also established that the physical thinning of grey matter that usually comes with ageing had actually been remarkably diminished.

• Researchers from UCLA found that when people become aware of their anger and label it as 'anger' then the part of the brain that generates negative emotions, the amygdala, calms down. It's almost as if once the emotional message has been delivered to the conscious mind it can quieten down a little.

• Mindfulness activates the 'rest and digest' part of our nervous system, and increases blood flow to parts of our brains that help us regulate our emotions, such as the hippocampus, anterior cingulate cortex and the lateral parts of the prefrontal cortex. Our heart rate slows, our respiration slows and our blood pressure drops. A researcher from Harvard coined the changes in the body that meditation evokes as the 'relaxation response' – basically the opposite to the 'stress response'. While the stress response is extremely detrimental to the body, the relaxation response is extremely salutary and is probably at the root of the wide-ranging benefits mindfulness has been found to have, both mentally and physically.

Mindfulness and the Body

- Researchers from the University of Wisconsin-Madison investigated the effects of mindfulness on immune system response. They injected participants with a flu virus at the end of an eight-week course and they found that the mindfulness group had a significantly stronger immune system compared with the others.

- Scientists at UCLA found mindfulness to be extremely effective at maintaining the immune system of HIV sufferers. Over an eight-week period, the group who weren't taught mindfulness had a 25% fall in their CDT 4 cells (the 'brains' of the immune system) whereas the group taught mindfulness maintained their levels.

- Researchers from the University of California, Davis, found that improved psychological well-being fostered by meditation may reduce cellular ageing. People who live to more than 100 have been found to have more active telomerase, an enzyme involved in cell replication. The researchers found that the meditators had a 30% increase in this enzyme linked to longevity following a three-month retreat.

- Skin disorders are a common symptom of stress. The University of Massachusetts taught mindfulness to psoriasis sufferers and found their skin problems cleared four times faster than those who weren't taught the technique.

- Researchers from the University of North Carolina have found mindfulness to be an effective method of treating irritable bowel syndrome. Over a period of eight weeks, participants either were taught mindfulness or they went to a support group. Three months later, they found that on a standard 500-point IBS symptom questionnaire, the support group's score had dropped by 30 points. The mindfulness group's score had fallen by more than 100 points.

- Researchers from Emory University investigated whether training in compassion meditation could reduce physiological responses to stress. Participants were stressed by being requested to perform a public speaking task. The researchers found that the participants who had practised the most had the lowest physiological responses to stress, as measured by reduced pro-inflammatory cytokines and also reported the lowest levels of psychological distress.

- Researchers investigated the physiological effects of an eight-week mindfulness programme on patients suffering from breast cancer and prostate cancer. In addition to the patients reporting reduced stress, they found significant reductions in physiological markers of stress, such as reduced cortisol levels, pro-inflammatory cytokines, heart rate and systolic blood pressure. A follow-up study a year later found these improvements had been maintained or enhanced further.

Mindfulness and Emotions

- Researchers from the University of Massachusetts Medical School investigated the effects of an eight-week mindfulness course on generalized anxiety disorder. 90% of those taught the technique reported significant reductions in anxiety.

- Studies from the University of Wisconsin suggest that meditators' calmness is not a result of becoming emotionally numb – in fact they may be able to experience emotions more fully. If asked to enter into a state of compassion, then played an emotionally evocative sound, such as a woman screaming, they showed increased activity in the emotional areas of the brain compared to novices. However, if asked to enter into a state of deep concentration, they showed reduced activity in the emotional areas of the brain compared with novices. The key is that they were better able to control their emotional reactions depending on the mental state they chose to be in.

- Optimists and resilient people have been found to have more activity in the front of their brains (prefrontal cortex) on the left hand side, whereas those more prone to rumination and anxiety have more on the right. Researchers from the University of Wisconsin found that after eight weeks of mindfulness practice, participants had been able to change their base-line levels of activity moving more towards left hand activation. This suggests that mindfulness can help us change our base-line levels of happiness and optimism.

- If you suffer from recurring depression, scientists suggest that mindfulness might be a way to keep you free from it. Researchers from Toronto and Exeter in the UK recently found that learning mind-fulness, while tapering off anti-depressants, was as effective as remaining on medication.

- Researchers from Stanford University have found that mindfulness can help with social anxiety by reducing reactivity in the amygdala, an area of the brain that is typically overactive in those with anxiety problems.

- Researchers at the University of Manchester tested meditators' response to pain, by heating their skin with a laser. They found that the more meditation the subject had done, the less they experienced pain. They also found that they had less neural activity in the anticipation of pain than controls, which is likely to be due to their increased ability to remain in the present rather than worry about the future.

- A recent study from Wake Forest University found that just four sessions of 20 minutes mindfulness training a day reduced pain sensitivity by 57% – an even greater reduction than drugs such as morphine.

- Numerous studies have found that mindfulness on its own or in combination with medication can be effective in dealing with addictive behaviours, from drug abuse through to binge eating. Recently researchers from Yale School of Medicine found that mindfulness training of less than 20 minutes per day was more effective at helping smokers quit than the American Lung Association's gold standard treatment. Over a period of four weeks, on average, there was a 90% reduction in the number of cigarettes smoked from 18 per day to two per day with 35% of smokers quitting completely. When they checked four months later over 30% had maintained abstinence.

- Researchers investigated the impact of mindfulness on the psychological health of 90 cancer patients. After seven weeks of daily practice, the patients reported a 65% reduction in mood disturbances including depression, anxiety, anger and confusion. They also reported a 31% reduction in symptoms of stress and less stress-related heart and stomach pain.

- Researchers from the University of California, San Diego investigated the impact of a four-week mindfulness programme on the psychological well-being of students, in comparison to a body relaxation technique. They found that both techniques reduced distress, however mindfulness was more effective at developing positive states of mind and at reducing distractive and ruminative thoughts. This research suggests that training the mind with mindfulness delivers benefits over and above simple relaxation.

Mindfulness and Thoughts/Cognition

- Researchers from Wake Forest University investigated how four sessions of 20 minutes mindfulness practice could affect critical cognitive abilities. They found that the mindfulness practitioners were significantly better than the control group at maintaining their attention and performed especially well at stressful tasks under time pressure. [This is another study demonstrating that significant benefits can be enjoyed from relatively little practise.]

- Researchers from the University of Pennsylvania wanted to investigate how mindfulness could help improve thinking in the face of stress. So, they taught it to marines prior to their deployment in Iraq. In cognitive tests, they found that the marines who practised for more than 10 minutes a day managed to maintain their mental abilities in spite of a stressful deployment period, whereas the control group and those practising less than 10 minutes could not.

- Researchers from UCLA conducted a pilot to investigate the effectiveness of an eight-week mindfulness course for adults and adolescents with ADHD. Over 75% of the participants reported a reduction in their total ADHD symptoms, with about a third reporting clinically significant reductions in their symptoms of more than 30%.

- Researchers conducted a pilot study, to investigate the efficacy of mindfulness in treating OCD. Sixty per cent of the participants experienced clinically significant reductions in their symptoms, of over 30%. The researchers suggest that the increased ability to 'let go' of thoughts and feelings helps stop the negative rumination process that is so prevalent in OCDs.

I hope the above has not put you to sleep but for me it makes me feel I'm in well-researched hands. If it's good enough for Harvard, UCLA, University of Pennsylvania, Yale School of Medicine and Stanford, it's good enough for me.

Summation

I've been practising and studying mindfulness for quite a while now. It's helped me to decrease the volume of the voices, defuse the onslaughts of self-recrimination and control my rage at others. Ten, twenty years ago, I imagined that I would be very depressed to say the least when I got to this age but I am happier or at least more content than I have ever been before. Here's how my life has changed so far:

Miracle 1

I have not passed the recordings of self-abuse to my children. I married my husband for his genes; he is that English type whose relatives not only survived the Blitz but they had a 'bloody jolly time' in it and still talk of the experience with fondness. Unlike me, my kids are not consumed by envy. Both daughters have friends who are already successful or getting prestigious jobs and guess what their reaction is? They are happy for them. They make collages with photos of their happy moments together; they are overjoyed for their friends. A miracle. When anyone ever got in my way when I was a child (which was pretty much everyone) I made plans to cut them open and remove their hearts.

Miracle 2

I am not, as my father predicted, a heroin addict by age 50. He would not listen to me when I said that people who shoot heroin usually start earlier, because he knew better. By 50, I would be a 'bum' and shooting heroin. So the miracle is that, against all his clairvoyant predictions, I'm not howling like a werewolf to the winds like my mother and, though I have depression, I have built a verbal castle wall around myself. My mantra is, 'I have an illness. I am not stupid, crazy, brain-damaged, slow, a failure, a moron. I simply have an illness.'

Miracle 4 (I missed 3 because I have dyslexia)
I got into the Royal Shakespeare Company. No explanation, I was not very talented but had the drive of a Rottweiler.

Miracle 5
I got into Oxford and completed my master's degree. (See explanation above.)

Miracle 6
Before the last egg left the building and against all odds, I got not one but three 'normalish' children.

Miracle 7
My daughters are the prom queens I always wanted to be; everyone returns their calls, they are invited to every party, they are surrounded by friends who love them, they are not eaten up by ambition and they do not know what it feels like to be left out.

Miracle 8
I did a TED Talks Global. I shat in my pants but I did it.

Miracle 9
I am writing a book and by this time hopefully have finished it or you're looking at blank pages.

Miracle 10

I had a pretty good career in entertainment until the breakdown.

So, HAHAHAHAHAHAHAHAHA to all my teachers who gave me 'D's in high school. HAHAHAHAHAHAHA to my parents who claimed I was slightly retarded. HAHAHAHAHA to all the people who tortured me in the playground.

(Sorry if this appears too narcissistic but I still carry some of that particular juice.)

Part Five

Alternative Suggestions
for Peace of Mind

The Manual

I try to practise some type of mindfulness for around 20 minutes when I get up in the morning, for five to ten minutes when I notice I'm tipping toward destructive thinking and a lot of five second bursts when I just want to stand back and notice what's going on. I use it now where in the past I would have popped a Xanax. It's an on-going process, not a miracle cure, but I would call myself at this point 'a recovered ruminator'. I still wake up with the impulse to leap upright from my bed with my demented to-do list, i.e. the compulsion to return a candle I bought six years ago. Nowadays the instructions are less burning and I don't always obey the commands. I still think about the candle but won't necessarily hunt through my receipts to prove I bought it. We have no bouncer at the doors of our mind to discriminate what gets into our consciousness and what doesn't, so some days it's like an over-crowded disco in my brain and I just have to sit it out, letting it 'party on' while underneath trying to track the feel of my breath. If I can sense even one single inhale or exhale, I've accomplished a great feat.

If I didn't have mindfulness, I would never stop the emailing until death do us part. For me mindfulness works, for others it might not. I don't like yoga; friends of mine can't stop (especially Bikram where you boil your bones to bend them). I would rather shoot myself than jog (I've ground my knees down to my ankles trying to do it); others can't live without it. Many people have their particular 'thing' that helps them cope with the on-going battle in their brains, so who am I to say what would work for them?

We All Need an Anchor We Can Lean On

If mindfulness isn't for you, I'm going to suggest some alternative practices to help you deal with everything from life's little hiccups to the gale force 10, brain-shattering breakdowns.

The important thing is that you find something to anchor you down when the winds of 'shit happens' get rough. So many people I know don't have an antidote for life's turbulent weather and suffer because of it. They ask me, 'Should I leave my husband? Change jobs? Stop eating cheese? Take up alcoholism?' Why, if we're still breathing and eating, is there such unhappiness? Dissatisfaction is part of the deal of living because simple existence is full of contradictions; we want individuality, to stand out from the crowd, yet we want be part of a tribe. We're driven and busy and yet we want peace. And worst of all, we want things to stay the same despite the fact that everything changes (that's the ultimate bummer). Why, oh, why can't we remain young or stay in love forever? You can't. Impermanence is the law of the universe – no can do. Even if you rage through the night, before you finish reading this sentence, billions of your cells have died and been reborn. Because we have consciousness, we suffer about the fact that we suffer and this second arrow of suffering is constructed in our brains. But if our brain can create this pain, it can also create happiness.

The skill required to tame your mind is to be able to inhibit your attention on certain things and intentionally take your focus to others. This is self-regulation, becoming the captain of the ship, steering your attention where you want it to be. An expert at self-regulation would be able to stay calm even in the face of my mother during one of her episodes.

When you find your particular practice, you'll have found not only *the manual* but also your ticket to your version of happiness.

Why Learning to Pay Attention is Important

Attention is like a spotlight and what it illuminates streams into your mind, so developing control over it is the most powerful way to shape your brain.

I can hear you say, 'What's with attention? I pay it when I cross the street.' No, for most of us, we are there physically but our attention could be in Sri Lanka. There is a big difference between experiencing something and being aware. The word 'experience' comes from the Latin 'experiri', meaning 'to try'. The word 'awareness' comes from the Greek 'horan', which means 'to see'. (I looked this up I don't automatically know these things). Experience is just showing up even though your mind is elsewhere, awareness is when you notice you're there.

We don't naturally pay attention, we have to learn it (see glitch in evolutionary development). The tragedy of most of our lives is that we're asleep at the wheel and no one tells us how to wake up. They say to kids at school, 'Pay attention'. How would they know how to do that? No one teaches them.

Scientists now have the technology to be able to trace what people's eyes focus on when they scan a room. Who or what an individual seeks out is based on genes, chemicals, culture, relationships and experience. What your eyes fasten onto is where your mind is in any one moment. Some people enter a room and zoom in on a daddy figure (nice but not sexy) or a sugar daddy (same, but with expensive shoes).

We become the character we are at any particular moment depending on what we focus on. On the golf course, swinging the club, you're a sportswoman. In bed in your nightie, you might be a sex kitten. With your kids you may be Mother Goose. (God help you if you ever get these roles confused.) These identities are all transitory; they come and go depending on which metaphorical clothes you wear and for what occasion.

You are where your attention is at any moment. An fMRI scanner can pick up the different neuronal patterns created when you focus on different objects and their patterns determine how and what you think.

We're living in a society that encourages multi-tasking; all interruptions by phones, texts, emails or other 'luminous rectangles' are welcome and what's more make us feel warm and wanted. 'I'm busy, therefore I am.' (A slight twist on the Descartes line.) Brain research shows that rather than it being a great accomplishment of mankind to be able to 'juggle everything', it may actually scramble your brain. (Duh!) The part of the brain you need for learning and memory, the hippocampus, is only active during uninterrupted focus. Interruptions of attention impair learning so if you're trying to learn Mandarin while speed walking on a treadmill, forget about it; it won't stick. You need focused attention to grow neural connections in the hippocampus, that's how learning happens. Focused attention builds up grey matter in the brain, which increases the ability to remember, attend, inhibit and execute actions, no matter what age you are.

Another reason attention is the road to freedom is that it allows you to see things as if for the first time and novelty is a component of happiness. If you actually taste, smell or touch something as if for the first time, you feel alive, excited and rediscover that sense of wonderment you had as a child when everything gave you a buzz. If you see the world through curiosity rather than a 'seen it, done it' lens then you'll notice things you never noticed before even if you've driven down the same road a thousand times. When you experience novelty, neurogenesis takes place (more neurons connect and make thicker clusters of information). I know that, if it was easy to pay attention, we'd all be able to snap out of our reverie at will. We'd all be able to intentionally 'smell the roses', which is an expression I find very irritating because who has time to do that?

The reason we don't visit the present too often is because evolution dictated that if we spent too much time in the moment, our survival would be in jeopardy. What if you're 'smelling the roses' and some predator comes up behind you? You'd be like, 'so dead'. This constant trawling the past to make sure we have a future is what keeps us alive. Awareness in the present can only be fleeting, maybe that's the beauty of it. Eventually your mind will always drag you where it needs to be; scanning the horizon with seemingly discon-nected, inconsequential streams of consciousness. This is our tragedy. You might be in the midst of watching the opening ceremony of the Olympics, jaw on the floor and still your mind will drag you back to, 'Why didn't my mother let me get a real Christmas tree? My bra had those foam cups in it where did I leave them? I will never forgive Dagmar Stuart for stealing my Barbie Doll's cocktail dress. I have to buy shampoo, I hate my feet, is it too late to take up pot-holing?' This cacophony of senseless banality is our destiny, our curse. But you can break this circuit; when you begin to train your attention; unwiring old patterns and re-wiring new ones, you promote *neuroplasticity*. Whatever you practice, you have to train regularly; only with repetition can you unwire the old habits and rewire the new.

Cognitive Behavioural Therapy (CBT)

Cognitive Behavioural Therapy was originally conceived by Dr Aaron T. Beck who began in the mid-1950s giving patients a means to observe their thoughts and beliefs and how they influence their moods and behaviours. CBT trains you to notice when your thinking is distorted so you can eventually stand back and question its validity.

Say you're meeting a guy for a blind date and he doesn't show up. You may think this means he's found out who you are and as a result finds you so hideous, he's ditched out. Cognitive therapy would help you to re-think your reaction and introduce the possibility that you over-reacted and that maybe he got the wrong address or just over-slept. With CBT you learn to test the usefulness and meaning of various thoughts you have and to change the thinking patterns that holds you locked in dysfunctional behaviours, moods and relationships. It may stop you from yelling, when you do meet up with the no-show date, 'I know that you're disgusted by me but I find you repulsive too.' You will have lost your dignity and he will have no idea what you're talking about.

CBT can be used for low self-confidence, guilt, stress, depression, apathy, the break-up of relationships, pressure at school, phobias and the inability to move on from the fact you lost the egg and spoon race at age eight. Anytime, in fact, where you're stuck in habitual thinking, feeling or behaving. The theory is that your thoughts, moods, behaviours and physical reaction are all interconnected in that they affect each other like falling dominos; your thinking affects your moods, which affect your behaviour, and vice versa. If you change how you think, it affects how you physically feel, which changes how you behave, which changes your mood.

CBT also illustrates the fact that negativity is nearly always based on distortions of thinking; it's what makes you feel worthless, dumb, helpless etc. A depressed mind filters out anything that contradicts the negative onslaught. Fewer phone calls or finding out about a party you haven't been invited to could trigger feelings of rejection that might drive you to hide in your bed for a week. You will remain lost unless you do something about it i.e. change your thinking. All of us have our own homemade package of distorted thinking ready to bring out whenever we feel threatened or stressed.

Examples of Distorted Thinking

1. **All or Nothing Thinking –** When you evaluate a situation you see it as either black or white; no grey in sight, even though we all know there are 57 shades.

2. **Overgeneralization –** Here you randomly come to the conclusion that if something happens to you it will happen again and again. You will notice if you're suffering from this syndrome because your sentences will start with, 'This always happens . . .', 'This is typical . . .', 'Every time I do that it happens . . .', 'This stuff only happens to me . . .'. Sound familiar? Welcome to overgeneralization (my world).

3. **Mental Filter –** You see everything in the world as not being even as a glass half empty but as a glass completely broken into a million pieces on the floor and you'll probably cut your foot on one of the shards.

4. **Disqualifying the Positive** – A magical trick where, before your very eyes, you can transform a positive experience, hey presto, into a negative one. This is where any compliment is seen as a fiction invented for ulterior motives. When I got into Oxford, I assumed it was because they were just after my money for the enrolment fees (this still might actually be true). When I was in a mental institution for my depression, I assumed the staff members were only being nice because of the massive fees I was paying and that they really hated me.

5. **Jumping to Conclusions** – Also called 'mind-reading'. If I look out at an audience and notice one person with their head down or eyes not pointing at me, I know immediately I have flopped and probably will flop for the rest of my life.

6. **Magnification and Minimization** – This is another favourite of mine. It occurs when you either blow things up or shrink them down depending on which-ever one is more hurtful. So you awfulize your dramas and hardly mention the award you won.

7. **Emotional Reasoning** – This is the one where you think that your emotions are telling you the truth. So because you often say you're stupid, you must there-fore have something wrong in your brain. My mother used to tell me she thought something was wrong with my brain because she imagined she was contaminated by some chemical that was released just before she escaped from Austria. (I do not know what chemical she was referring to but she stood by her beliefs.)

8. **Should/Ought/Must Statements –** These are very popular for everyone. The inner voice thinks it's helping by adding, 'I must have . . . [fill in anything]' to supplement your supply of self-loathing. Some people call it 'musturbation'.

9. **Labelling and Mislabelling –** This could also be called 'overgeneralization', when you smack a label on yourself and believe it. If you win a silver medal in the 400 metres at the Olympics and then call yourself a loser, you might be mislabelling.

10. **Personalization –** You imagine everything is your fault even when you had nothing to do with it. There's an earthquake, it has nothing to do with your bad moods. My phone used to break constantly, I believed it picked up my anger and hormonal rage and that the crackle of my vibes killed it.

Doing CBT – The Homework

Your CBT therapist will give you homework each week and encourage you to record your reactions and note down alternative responses to particular situations that push your buttons. The recording of your thoughts, moods and physical feelings gives you distance, which allows you to have objectivity when you're testing their validity. There are a myriad of different CBT exercises. Here is just one example.

The Situation
Who?
What?
When?
Where?

Moods
Depressed
Sad
Ashamed
Guilty
Frightened
Panicky
Happy
Hurt
Scared
Nervous
Humiliated

I'm sure you have your own theme song.

Alternative Suggestions for Peace of Mind

Rating Moods

After you identify each mood you experience, you rate its intensity and by doing this you begin to notice how your moods fluctuate.

Rate from 0 – 100
0 – No feeling at all
100 – The most you've ever felt

Automatic Thoughts

What was going through your mind just before you started to feel this way? Any other thoughts? Images? By using this exercise, you may start to notice themes and these are your automatic thoughts. For example:

Everyone hates me
I don't deserve this
I'm a failure
I'm going to get caught
I'm a loser
I'm being taken advantage of
People are lying to me

Physical Sensations

Nausea
Cramping
Butterflies
Wind (not good in meetings)
Pounding in the heart
Shakiness
Weakness
Dizziness

Numbness
Tingling
Vomiting (also not good in meetings)

Alternative/Balanced Thoughts

Is there an alternative way of thinking about the situation?

If you were with a friend who asked for advice because this was happening to her, how would you help her deal with the situation?

Action Plans

These are to help you solve the problems that you've identified. Write as many helpful suggestions as you can think of to move forward in the eventuality of a similar situation. Write as if you were advising a friend.

Rate Moods Now

After filling in the CBT Spreadsheet, re-rate moods listed in the MOODS column as well as any new moods on a scale from 0 to 100% based on intensity.

Example of CBT Spreadsheet – Fill in Your Own

SITUATION	MOODS	RATING MOODS 0-100%	AUTOMATIC THOUGHTS
Who? What? When? Where?	Examples: Sad Hurt Anxious		Examples: I'm a failure No one likes me I should have . . .

EXAMPLE OF CBT SPREADSHEET – FILL IN YOUR OWN

PHYSICAL SENSATIONS	ALTERNATIVE/ BALANCED THOUGHTS	ACTION PLANS	RATE MOODS NOW 0-100%
Examples: Nausea Heart pounding	Examples: Don't sweat the small stuff You did the best you could	Examples: Next time get professional help Take a holiday	

My Personal CBT Spreadsheet

Situation

A while back, I found myself driving at top speed to get to an appointment on time for something so shallow I don't even want to mention it. The appointment for this shallow thing was at 11 a.m. I had arranged for a plumber to come over between 9.30 and 10.30 a.m. to fix my boiler. I would have to leave at the latest at 10.15 a.m. to make my appointment. He arrived at 10.10 a.m. (which is a miracle in itself) but I was now going to be late. He took a long time gazing at my boiler and then did what plumbers do best, told me an endless fairytale about how my cylinder was already out of date in the Dark Ages and I'd need a replacement. At 10.40 a.m. I decided I had to take a shower (based on insanity). In the rush, I forgot to open the shower door, banged into it and had a nosebleed. As I dressed quickly, I ripped my underwear trying to get both legs in one hole. At 10.50 a.m., I got into my car and drove down a one-way street, giving the finger to oncoming cars driving past me.

Just a note: I think I inherited this addiction to lateness and giving myself an adrenaline rush from my mother who used to hunt for dustballs under the sofa while my dad was honking the horn to drive her to the airport. Once she arrived in the UK with no luggage, only the dress on her back but dammit she got that dust ball before she left and in the world of OCD that was all that mattered.

Moods and Rating of Intensity

Self-loathing 85%
Panicked 95%

Furious 92%
Frustrated 75%
Nervous 99%

Automatic Thoughts
Mainly Devil voices. 'I'm a f— up, sh— cu— fu— ass—
wipe— cu—. I'm getting my nails painted, my f—king nails!'
(That was what the appointment was for.) 'I'm so ashamed,
most of the rest of the world are dying and I'm having the
tips of my fingers painted. And worse I'm going to drive over
people and kill them to have it done.'

Physical Sensations
Sweat dripping off my face and neck
Hard and quick breathing, then no breathing at all
Heart like a drum solo at a heavy metal concert
Forehead held in vice grip.

Alternative/Balanced Thoughts
1. Screaming will not make you move any faster.

2. Take off your watch and hide it. Looking at your
   watch continuously won't make you move any faster.

3. At a stoplight think to yourself that's it far better to
   stay alive than to have blue nails. You can have blue
   nails when you're dead.

4. Try and bring some awareness to your body and send
   relaxation to areas you notice might be a little tight.

> Uncurl your toes
> Un-wrench your neck
> Un-hump your shoulders
> Unclench your jaw
> Smile

5. Do not get angry at yourself for this highly-pressured incident. Just say, 'I'm going to plan better next time' and give yourself a little hug. (A little irony went on there if you remember my views on hugging – not great.)

Action Plans

Next time you arrange it, make the appointment with the plumber at another time, another day or year but not minutes before you need to go somewhere. Get yourself a lovely calendar with lilies on it and write down your appointments. When you have completed them, give yourself a gold star next to the date.

Put an X with tape on your shower door so you don't bang into it again.

Maybe think about how unnecessary it is to paint your nails blue in the big scheme of things.

Intensity of Moods Now

25% (Ta-da!)

Do not, I repeat do not punish yourself for being late or say to yourself, 'I screwed up again,' 'It's my parents' fault.' You have probably been someone who's late for a long time. If you try to figure out why, throw out the welcome mat to rumination.

My Story

ANOTHER EXAMPLE OF MY ANXIETY TRIGGERS
I have invited guests for dinner and it's now one hour before they arrive. I'm frantically fingering though my stain-covered collection of cookbooks that I never use. The words mean nothing to me and the photos are too intimidating, reminding me of my inability to do anything domestic. If I actually tuned into what I'm thinking it would be total contempt for the people I've invited over. The minute they said, 'Yes' to my invitation, I resented them for making me go through this. I know that I invited them but I hate them now and I hate myself for inviting them.

Half an hour before the guests arrive, I decide to call people who can cook to help me. (Once I even called Nigella who thought I was joking and hung up.) I have now started to call random people in my 'contacts', offering any amount of cash if they will come over and cook dinner for the 12 friends I will never speak to again. When that fails, I will get in my car, in full hunting mode and drive up and down the street, looking frantically out of the window as if someone is going to come up to me with a tray full of ready-cooked meals.

Ten minutes before guest time, I have found myself running up and down the aisles of a super-market not knowing what goes with what and then hurling myself before a butcher begging for him to tell me how and what to stuff a lamb chop with because these are fancy people coming over. You can't just throw them a plain lamb chop, it has to be something stuffed; this makes me hate them even more. As the butcher explains, I have no idea what he's talking about but write it down with shaking hands. I'm still trying to call Nigella on my mobile but she's not answering.

I drive home swerving to avoid killing off whole families, then into the kitchen turning on the oven, realizing it doesn't heat up right away so I do what I always do – scream at the oven to hurry up – and then the doorbell rings. I shriek through the intercom, 'Come in, just a minute', then run upstairs tripping several times, tearing off my clothes and take that crucial shower I always take when I'm really in a hurry. I slide out, smashing into the same shower door, wipe some eye shadow near my eye, grab any clothes, fall down the stairs and open the door, try to sound casual while noticing I'm wearing something crumpled I just took out of the laundry basket.

Then I realize with complete horror that I've forgotten to buy any finger foods for them to nibble on (God I hate that word). I skip backwards into the kitchen opening the cabinets so hard one of the doors falls off and find some old ham and peanut butter and (luckily) toothpicks. I begin to rip the ham into squares, stick the toothpicks in and smear just a little peanut butter on top. I open my fridge and to my delight find an olive and add it to the ham/peanut butter hors d'oeuvres.

The rest of the evening is a travesty because I've

thrown wine back into my mouth so fast, I do a monologue without noticing no one is laughing or even listening. After an hour or two I'm still going, telling stories repeatedly with no punch-line. Doing a CBT spreadsheet might have been very useful.

MY WEDDING

I couldn't find the ring that Ed bought me, and it was the morning of my wedding. We were going to be married in a registry office because I had been married twice before: once to a gay person, to get a work permit for me to work in the UK, and another time to get a work permit for another gay person to help him work in America. The magic of a white wedding, needless to say, had been sucked out of me.

With hardly any notice, I invited everyone the day before and when I got to the registry office (late), as we walked toward the registrar, I whispered to Ed how old I really was and that I'd been married twice before – had he known before the event he might have tried to bolt. Due to my lateness, I couldn't find the wedding ring so I just grabbed the receipt, and wrapped it around my finger for all to see and admire the actual price. It was a travesty.

Not Everyone is Late

There are people in the world – I've heard rumours, it may be true – who actually appear at events and appointments early but I cannot relate to them so I won't write about them. Perhaps being early could be another type of distorted thinking. The action is propelled by another kind of nagging voice, 'I can't be late. If I'm late no one will respect/like/love me.' Whichever way you go, late or early, it definitely disturbs your wellbeing.

My Problem with CBT

CBT works for so many people, I don't want to throw a spanner in the works but I thought I'd throw in my opinion, which is always a spanner. If you're continually digging up thoughts and feelings even though you're standing back and noting them down, they might spark off self-critical and repetitive, negative thinking, which are forerunners of an assault of depression.

It's words that keep you captive in your head so remembering and documenting perpetuates the voices. To put everything into words means the mind has to travel to the past, thereby strengthening past and future thinking pulling you out of experiencing the present.

Evidence of How Mindfulness Produces Better Results Than CBT

John Teasdale, who helped develop MBCT, tested the efficacy of mindfulness compared with CBT on a group of clinically-depressed patients in remission. He found that the relapse rate into another depressive episode differed dramatically. 62% of patients given traditional CBT relapsed as against 36% of those who did MBCT. The researchers measured metacognition and those who could achieve it were the ones least likely to relapse.

EXERCISE – SELF-REGULATION WITH THE TRAFFIC SIGNAL GAME

Emotional Intelligence

Self-regulation is beginning to be taught to kids at primary schools, alongside the academic syllabus. (About time.) Think of the advantages these kids will have over us. They learn before they send blame (or start to bully, or think the world is unfair) how their own emotions work, which for some strange reason has never been taught before or hardly mentioned, as far as I know.

Traffic Signals

When a child feels he is leaving his neutral (calm) zone and heading towards stress, fear, anxiety, sadness or panic, he holds up a RED CARD.

All other people are not allowed to come within a six feet radius, they are told to just leave him alone.

When the child feels his stress levels coming down, he holds up a YELLOW CARD.

When he feels he is back to his base-line of calm he holds up a GREEN CARD.

Now the teacher helps him process what went on for him. He learns to understand what he's bringing into the room instead of projecting it out onto other people, believing that they caused his feelings. He may well be reacting to others but they did not cause his emotions; only he can create them and only he can reduce them. So he has learnt to regulate his feelings.

Imagine how useful this would be in an office when a meeting gets emotionally hot. When people lose their neutral base-line of calm and the emotional temperatures get too high, the rest of the meeting is a waste of time and energy. When people 'LOCK ANTLERS' they get into a fight mode; the original argument goes out the window and now it's just biological warfare. (Your biology.) The people involved literally go OUT OF THEIR MINDS; their memory goes down because cortisol is now killing off neurons in the hippocampus, blood leaves the brain, breathing becomes shallow, stopping oxygenation in the brain and now they're looking for a fight not a solution.

How great it would be if we as adults could recognize when we're heading towards a melt-down, hold up the RED CARD or even just a WHITE FLAG of surrender that says, 'Meeting over, I'm crazy right now, I'll be back when I'm normal.'

Alternative Suggestions for Peace of Mind

Imagine how many wars we could avoid if we knew we were aware that we're carrying the dynamite (our own emotions) and knew how to back off. If we could recognize that we might be the weapons of mass destruction ourselves all would be well in the world.

Maybe this could spread to world leaders, when they get hot under the collar, they'd know to hold up the RED CARD and everyone would stay six feet away from them until their hissy fit was over and then when they'd feel sane again, they'd hold up a GREEN CARD. That would be a world without war.

If we had a MANUAL which I've been going on about for a while, it would instruct you that if you're going to an interview, audition, business meeting, head-to-head with your friends or family in a highly-charged state, back off and come back later; otherwise it will only end in tears.

EXERCISE – RE-DECORATING YOUR INSIDES

If you're feeling overwhelmed by stress, worry, anger, fear write down at least three situations or moments you consider to be positive, however small. Emotions are as transient as pain; write down when you have a moment where you notice a feeling that might be, dare I say it, positive. Write down the situation when you felt this positive feeling, along with the date and time.

Example:

13 September 16:04 – Someone smiled at me on the bus. Got a twinge of lightness and heart twang of happiness. (Don't write, 'They probably thought I was someone else.')

11 November 14:37 – My cat sat on my lap and I felt velvet in my chest.

24 December 8:00 – I saw a red Christmas bauble and was pinged with pleasure. (No one will see your journal so don't be embarrassed by how schmaltzy you might sound.)

All of this is to build up a storage space of memories of feeling good that you can call up at will. When you become aware of these breaks in the weather, your brain is unwiring from the embedded negative patterns and each time you're aware of a positive sensation the brain fires with new patterns. (Building more positive muscles.)

EXERCISE – SELF-REGULATION USING SMELL

I have a friend who told me there's a candle with a scent called 'Winter' that reminds her of Christmas when she was a child: part warm, gingerbread cookies, part pine trees. She told me that whenever she smells it she feels she's in the body of her ten-year-old self and a feeling of sweetness spreads throughout her body; she feels her shoulders melt down and her eyes go soft. Before a meeting or appointment that's unnerving, she brings out the candle and sniffs it when no one's looking and the soothing feeling returns. She goes into the meeting in this open and relaxed state, able to take the bumps; her mind calm so she can think clearly, creatively and quickly. If she suddenly gets a spike of anxiety she excuses herself, goes to the ladies' and sits there smelling the candle bringing herself back to neutral. This is self-regulating at its best; knowing how to manage your inner state and doing something about it.

EXERCISE – SELF-REGULATION USING SIGHT

I have a friend called Joanna who carries a photo of herself in mid-air on a zip wire. Whenever she brings it out to look at it, she's back up there, flying through the trees. When she knows she has to face some challenging event, she peeks at the picture. I once watched her give a speech on stage. I could tell when her confidence started to ebb because she'd glance at the lectern where I knew she had the photo. Each time she looked at it her whole body relaxed, her voice got stronger, her eyes relaxed and she got back her sense of humour. (That's the first thing to sink when you lose your nerve.) She told me that as soon as she senses a small stab of fear just knowing the photo is nearby gets her right back to that sense of freedom, flying in the trees.

This could be such a useful tool in business for presentations. I have watched big heads of organizations stand on stage giving their PowerPoint presentations with those graphs of success going up and down; meaning nothing to anyone. They may have the brains to be the CEO but they have no idea that they have put the whole audience into a coma; droning on and on about values or profits or who cares what – no one's listening. If they had a way of reading other people they might notice people nodding off and do something about it: change course, crack a joke or become human for a minute and say that they can see people aren't really responding and ask for any suggestions? Any of these alternatives to the coma-inducing state can win back an audience. People need to know that you know they're out there.

Alternatives

You could also prime your positive emotions with:

Sound – Listen to a piece of music before a stressful event (whatever rocks your boat). I have a recording of sounds from the jungle, parrots squawking and rain dripping – as soon as I listen to it, I'm on holiday, and my body goes calm. I don't care who's shouting at me in those moments.

Touch – Grab a swatch of cashmere that you like to touch (or leather for those of you who might be into leather) to bring you back to normal (whatever it means).

Taste – Feeling tense? Put a sweet in your mouth. (Choose something small or you'll just be chewing in someone's face forever, which will actually worsen the stress).

In the Brain

Using any one of sense-provoking stimuli can promote feelings of well being, which has physiological repercussions: you feel good, so you get an increase in dopamine to get that motivated feeling. (Just enough makes you feel positive and keen to accomplish things, too much and you're chasing your tail.)

When you intentionally use an image that calms you down, you're immediately lowering the amygdala, and rerouting activity to your prefrontal cortex, which promotes higher thinking and better decision-making. When you're in this positive state you're increasing neural growth; enhancing learning and more workspace in the memory.

Also, when you focus on something that brings out a positive reaction – your child's face or your cat curled up in a salad bowl (mine does that, it's adorable) – brain scanning shows that the areas that are responsible for calming you down become more activated. Whether you see something in actuality or picture it in your mind, the same area lights up in the brain. If you touch something warm, the same area in your brain lights up as when you feel emotional warmth. So simply by using images of things that make you feel good, you're activating the 'feel good' area. This is really USING YOUR BRAIN.

EXERCISE – OPENING YOUR LENS WITH NOVELTY

Using a journal, write down when you notice something you've seen for the first time. Start with three entries a day. For example:

My daughter has yellow in her green eyes.
That tree has buds on it.
I can hear a clock ticking from the next room.
My dog's bark is different from my neighbour's dog.
This blade of grass is greener than the other one.

Reminder: Novelty grows neurons.

EXERCISE – YOUR GRATITUDE

I used to make fun of a friend of mine called Kathy who told me she writes down a few things each day she's grateful for. I could never imagine doing that because I find it a bit frilly but she seems much calmer and happier these days, so who am I to say? She tells me that no matter how dark things get she will find that gap of light. For example:

I have two legs.

I can taste ice cream.

I am alive.

EXERCISE – LABELLING

My friend Tanya told me as soon as she recognizes one of her critical voices that's giving her hell, she labels it. This gives her distance from the onslaught.

She told me she was called back to a job interview four times and after the fourth was rejected. Rather than think, 'Well, I got close that time, I'll get a job at some point soon' (I have yet to meet someone who thinks like that), her habitual stab-in-her-own-back response was, 'I'm never going to get a job'. She told me as soon as she hears her familiar theme, she labels it as 'Worrying'.

When she starts to berate herself for failing, she labels it 'Berating'.

When she panics that she's never going to get a job, she labels it 'Panicking'.

When she starts creating scenarios where she's homeless and Prada-less, she labels it as 'Fantasizing' or 'Catastrophizing'. I would also call it 'Pradasizing'.

The labelling disidentifies the hot emotions and changes the relationship to the thoughts. If thoughts and feelings have labels, they are no longer some solid part of you but transient items that come and go at random. It's as if you're saying, 'Oh, that's anxiety' (out there) rather than 'I am anxious' (in me).

EXERCISE – NAMING THE DEMON

Whenever I used to get a sniff of rejection, I would slide straight back to the feeling I had as a child: lonely, ignored and a little freakish. The incident could be as minuscule as not being invited to a birthday party. I'd immediately jump to the conclusion that they had found out I was a freak from my childhood records.

Whenever I got that feeling, I gave it a name: Mitzi. I'd think, 'Ok, I'm now in the Mitzi mode'. I had a very distinct picture in my mind of her: ratty hair, a dirty face, scrawny and wearing rags. (Not dissimilar to a character in *Oliver* but with an American accent.) Whenever I'd feel that black hole of despair and rejection, I'd bring up the image of Mitzi, which in turn made me feel compassion for her (myself). I realized this is an eccentric way of dealing with depression. (I would go and write this up in a book and get it published but it turns out I am doing that.

Mitzi

EXERCISE – DEALING WITH MY OTHER DEMONS

Besides Mitzi I gave all my other demons a name.

Stella

When I get a bit of envy I picture Stella. She's blonde, wears a floaty white toga and has pointy teeth with blood on them. Stella pulls the pain right out of me and I can watch her objectively. She cries a lot so I sit her on my lap and console her and the agony passes.

Fred

When I used to get a whiff of anger, I feel myself transform like from a woman to a werewolf. I have a trigger finger when it comes to rage. In the past I'd even seek out situations where I could provoke people so I could vent my reptilian anger on them. I would hunt down innocent people (never friends). I'd find a snappy bus driver, a librarian who told me my book was over-due and tear into them until they were just a pile of bones. The fury was addictive and tasted delicious while I was in mid-spew, the problem was that hours later I'd suffer something like a serious hangover from all the poison I'd thrown about.

It all comes back to you. That is the lesson I learnt. I had to start to muzzle the beast and by giving it this image, I'd just watch it bark and snarl and spit until it was exhausted and then slink away whimpering. If I let it go it would just get too tired to continue. I never gave this image a name but it might have been even more helpful if I'd called him something harmless like 'Fred,' he would have been far less frightening.

Fred

EXERCISE – HABIT BREAKERS

Each tiny change of habit you make opens up a small chink in the wall you've built around yourself; keep on changing and you'll be able to break free from the prison you've created. SMALL STEPS MAKE BIG CHANGES.

The chair you're used to sitting on – change it.
The route you drive/walk/take a train to work – change it.
The type of people you like to be around – change them.
Sleep on the other side of the bed.
Change to another toothpaste/perfume/lipstick/soup.
(Maybe think twice before you change your husband/wife.)

EXERCISE – FAKING IT TO MAKE IT

I've heard your facial expressions can change how you feel. In one experiment researchers asked students to hold a pencil between their teeth in order to give them the physical appearance of smiling. They were then asked to rate their feelings while looking at neutral photos. The ones with the pencils said the photos made them feel good while those not smiling (pencil-less) said they made them feel either nothing or sad. Not only did the experiment evoke positive feelings in the person with the pencil, it created positive feelings in other people (mainly because they laughed at the people with the pencil in their mouths.)

Don't laugh, just smile and put a pencil in your mouth.

EXERCISE – TOTAL DISTRACTION

If emotions or thoughts get too hot, be good to yourself and just totally switch your attention to take down the heat. (Try not to pick something that will harm you, i.e. drugs, too much food or over-shopping.)

Start counting from 1 to 100 backwards
Watch television/a film
Listen to loud music
Read something shallow or this book
Run/walk/dance/swim . . .

EXERCISE – ATTENTIVE LISTENING AND TALKING – RAPPORT

To be done in pairs.

Step One

For one minute talk to each other.

Now turn your backs to each other and each person describe what colour eyes the other one has, what her hair is like (colour) and what the other is wearing. This helps us to realize how little we notice what's right in front of our eyes.

Step Two

Try again – take it in turns for each of you to talk to each other for another minute.

If you're the listener:

NOTICE What his body language is saying

His tone of voice

What words he/she chooses

What he might mean under the words

If you're the talker:

NOTICE How the other person is reacting to what you're saying

Alternative Suggestions for Peace of Mind

What emotions you're reading

When the other person looks like they want to say something

Step Three

Now both discuss what you were thinking and feeling i.e. any inner voices?

This is the best way to instantly bond with someone else.

Compassion and Kindness

'A human being experiences himself, his thoughts and feelings, as something separated from the rest . . . This delusion is a kind of prison for us . . . Our task must be to free ourselves from this prison by widening our circles of compassion to embrace all living creatures and the whole of nature in its beauty.'

Albert Einstein

The essence of neuroplasticity is that what you practise you'll cultivate. If you are cruel and spiteful, you'll become expert at getting even crueller and more spiteful. If you practise being compassionate, you'll become more compassionate. That's how our brains work; the way we think or feel determines our wiring and what chemicals are coursing through our veins. If you're thinking or feeling agitated or angry you're pumping adrenaline and cortisol. If you're feeling love or compassion you've got some of that good old oxytocin fuelling you. Again we limit ourselves by believing we're born a certain way and we'll always remain that way.

To change the brain, all you need to do is put effort in it. For some of us feeling positive is very challenging. I know how to do hurt but being nice has not been part of my repertoire. If having a feeling of kindness or compassion is vague, you need to familiarize yourself with how it feels in your body and mind. Over time and with practise you may go from a twinge to a full feeling. The point is still to experience feelings, even positive ones as transitory; they all pass so you're not aiming at holding onto a feeling of beatific bliss but of equanimity, of 'going with the flow'.

I don't want to steal ideas from Alcoholics Anonymous but when they say 'Accept the things you cannot change and change the things you can', I couldn't say it any better.

The opposite of self-criticism is self-compassion and this can be cultivated. If you bring to mind something that moves you – i.e. a bunny rabbit or your baby (no one will find out), notice how kindness and affection feel in your body. The feelings of kindness are an antidote for when you feel sad or depressed. If you're in that 'kindness' state, watch how your words and actions affect what you're doing or who you're talking to. These feelings spread out and when you feel good, others catch it and send it right back to you.

It's not so hard to send kindness to things and people you love. The more advanced course is when you deliberately send it to someone who has upset you or you don't like. If you can, the results are always positive and if you can't, just forgive yourself because letting yourself off the hook is also kindness.

A Story . . .

One evening, a Native American elder told his grandson about a battle that goes on inside people. He said, 'My son, the battle is between two wolves inside us all. One is anger, envy, jealousy, sorrow, regret, greed, arrogance, self-pity, guilt, resentment, inferiority, lies, false pride and superiority. The other is joy, peace, love, hope, serenity, humility, kindness, benevolence, empathy, generosity, truth and compassion.' The grandson thought about it for a minute and then asked his grandfather, 'Which wolf wins?' The elder simply replied, 'The one that you feed.'

EXERCISE – SPORTS AND EXERCISE

Everyone knows exercise improves your health, longevity, physical and mental state, and generally makes you feel better in yourself. A hit of your own endorphins is almost better than any drug you can buy over or under the counter. My only problem with the blanket expression 'take exercise', is that most of us do it without thinking, we just jerk our bodies around, squat, push, kick or scrunch in the hope of a harder pec. You see people in the gym, running on the spot for hours, reading a book, watching the news, their minds millions of miles away from what their feet are doing. This could be called mindless exercise, which in the end does more damage than good. I've watched people do 1000 sit-ups in under two minutes knowing that they will very shortly pull every disc they've got. When I came to England in the 1970s, no one was even brushing their teeth, now they have to go to the gym every day before and after work. Men, and not just gay ones, suddenly need a six-pack. For what? In case they suddenly get cast to go topless on an aftershave ad? Suddenly everywhere there are these amphitheatres with hundreds of male and female bums grinding away to MTV; rock solid babes, their leotards lodged somewhere in their liver they're cut so high. On the running machines you see elderly people, hunched over, nearly dead but their little stick legs are moving just because the treadmill is still switched on; if they stop they'll be sucked under the belt never to be seen again, just a pair of false teeth left behind.

Many people use exercise to try to literally run away from their uncomfortable emotions or thoughts. Out they jump at 5 a.m. and do whatever they have to do to cut themselves off from their voices. The voices will eventually win out because when you can no longer run, pole vault or even walk (and I don't want to depress you but this will happen) your mind will still be in the state you left it. The bottom line is that *you have to exercise your brain as much as you do your body*.

Dance, jump, hump, flip, high-kick all you want when you're young, you're made to be bouncy but at a certain point, mindless exercise isn't good for you and you may rip something and hurt yourself very badly.

The idea is to be able to exercise the part of your body you want to exercise while everywhere else is relaxed – this is how you get toned not tensed. Again this is using intentional attention. A fit muscle is one that's strong but released, not stiff and contracted and you can only have that if you attend to the area you're working out.

These days, professional athletes are trained to sit still with their eyes closed and imagine the movements their muscles need to make when they're actually competing. Besides the actual physical training, they are virtually picturing their grip on the tennis racket, their arm lifting, the other arm throwing up the ball, slamming it down, etc and as they imagine these moves, neuronal connections are wiring together in the equivalent area of the motor cortex. When it comes to the actual play, they have primed the correct muscles so they'll be able to move faster and play harder in the real game. It's the mental training of attention, not pure physical training that increases memory and learning capabilities.

The best exercise is done when you're sensing what you're moving, flexing, lifting, pushing and pumping.

Alternative Suggestions for Peace of Mind

Some examples of mindful practises are:

Pilates

Yoga

Tai Chi

Qigong

Martial arts

All of these can be done mindlessly but part of the training is to make sure every move is sensed from the inside. Breath is used to connect the body and the mind and each move is closely observed moment-by-moment. The practices above are, in my opinion, mindfulness in movement: sharpening attention and focus, and bringing you to a state of calm and peace. On the other hand, when I do Zumba (I think I'm fantastic at this until I look in the mirror) I just let myself 'go with the flow' not really thinking about my breath or what my body is doing. (It's all about consciously choosing when you want automatic pilot and when you don't.)

Curiosity

This is what makes us superior. Sadly many people don't use it. They have it, but it has become obsolete. We are born with this feature, that's why when we're children, our hunger for information is insatiable, we don't even care what the story is, we just want to be stimulated. That is how our brains grow and how, as more and more neurons connect, we become smarter. Then comes school. The point of going is, hopefully, to ignite that nascent curiosity in more ways; history, math, religion, literature etc. Millions of years ago they didn't have school but it was a matter of life and death for the kids to learn how to make a fire, beat animals sense-less with rocks and wash their hands before they went to the loo.

These days, I feel that what kills the spark of curiosity is the fact that everything hangs on a grade. Nothing will burn out an interest quicker. I'm aware high grades get you into a great university where you will go to the best parties, but if you get hooked on this chasing the grade thing and (even worse) if your parents push you too hard, you might find that you get the habit of chasing a rabbit for the rest of your life, thinking that there will be some reward in front of you, always just out of reach. And when you conquer something, it might not be for the personal satisfaction of attaining a goal but rather for beating the competition.

So curiosity goes out the window and competitive spirit steps in. Again, you need it and it's not a bad trait but when you end up studying law when your passion is pottery, it's a sad state of affairs. True, we don't need so many pots and it's hard to sell them but at least you might experience satisfaction in your life, even though you'll probably need to be on welfare. If you do things simply for gaining more cash, fame, status, power or an A+, misery or madness lie in your path.

My final word on this is that only if you find something you love doing and then do it, is life worth living. I tell that to my daughters adding that they should marry someone rich who'll be able to afford the pursuit of their dreams. To me, the most important and beneficial of all exercises is the strengthening of your curiosity because that is the glue that binds the human race. If you are curious about someone else, and show it, it is the most flattering thing you can do for them; they will give you anything; the keys to their car, their business, they'll probably even marry you. I have a friend who decides in minutes if she wants to go on a date with someone by timing how long it takes him to say 'you' rather than 'I'. Most people don't ask questions and some of the most brilliant people I know (with IQs off the planet) have no curiosity and are therefore idiots.

If we practise how to attend to one other and not just win debates or show each other how much information we can stuff in our heads, we would evolve a truly civilized world. In business, if you learn to listen and be curious about another person and pay attention to how he feels, negotiations would be a breeze. Huge amounts of money, time and energy are wasted by people talking at each other rather than with each other. There should be training simply to learn how to be curious rather than endless MBA programs. People are what sells, nothing else. You like and trust the person, you'll do business with them and if you are genuinely curious, people won't be able to resist you. If you learn to speak and listen mindfully, stepping out of your habitual patterns of behaviour, you will reduce interpersonal conflicts, stereotyping and cross-cultural misunderstanding.

Summation

The main message of THE MANUAL is that change is all that we can be sure of, and our lives are uncertain. Holding on to anything only creates more suffering.

Everything changes all the time, from the volatility of quantum particles to every cell in our nervous system. Even our consciousness, probably located in our prefrontal cortex, is updated five to eight times a second. Thoughts come and go like each breath we take; they come, disperse and disappear.

Life is much more than scratching the itch of wanting something and 'chasing the dragon'. (See Jimmy Choo shoes) And if we can just become aware, once in a while, that our minds have taken us hostage to somewhere in the past or future and when they do remember to focus on what's really out there (sound, taste, touch, sight, smell or the breathing). The only thing keeping us from being present is our thoughts and thoughts aren't facts.

In order to survive, your brain fools you into making you believe that there are fixed patterns in this chaotic world and that we can actually create permanent plans. Our brains are constantly chasing after a moment that has just passed, trying to control it. It's like taking a photo of a waterfall and believing it's actually stopped in time. Everything is gone before you even register it. It is now . . . and now it's gone and so in a sense everything is memory.

When you were a kid, those neurons were firing every second; everything was novel and exciting, you'd say things like, 'I want to be a fireman or an astronaut', with absolutely no consideration of qualifications required. (I wanted to be a mermaid.) Everything is possible – you can look at a snow-flake for hours and configure cloud clusters as neighbour-hoods. 'That cloud is my house and that one is my bedroom and I can jump to your cloud and visit and have tea.' Everything was fresh back then, in full living technicolour and you were excited out of your mind. You get older some asshole tells you, you can't be a mermaid, for whatever reason, or you can't fly like Superman. As you get older, your world gets tinier and tinier because you believe you don't have options until you die in a rut.

And no one seems to care that we end up growing into such a tiny part of our potential, we just think, 'Oh well, this is how I ended up'. We say about old people, 'Oh that's just Grandma' or 'Boo Poo', or 'Kree Kree', or whatever we're calling them now (when you're old you're treated like a pet). 'Oh, that's just Granny. She does the same thing every day – she has her tea at four, then walks her dog at five, naps at six and then beddy byes.'

This is how and why our brains atrophy, because we start to say the same thing over and over again without anyone telling you, 'Shut up you said that before'. When you're old you don't want to change chairs, countries, learn the tango, parachute jump (you're old – what's the worst that could happen?) Forget Sudoku or crossword puzzles, you're using the same parts over and over again when you do those and we're already too cognitively strong. Improvise your life, grow some new neurons. That's how everything becomes fresh again and you could even end up a mermaid.

Summation

And if you allow your thoughts to drive you and you believe that your reality is the same as everyone else's, you'll become hard, judgmental, intolerant and it will choke you in the end with bitterness. The lens through which you see yourself and your world will become more and more narrow, until it's dull and you're dull and your world is dull. But you need to realize that we are constantly in flux, and everything changes constantly, even you. You're always in a state of 'becoming'. There is no point in grabbing onto anything – people, money, clothes, stuff. No point. There is no safety anywhere because everything is the unknown.

And it does not matter how much you have to let go of. If you only end up with the gift of simply noticing things as if for the first time, notice their novelty, it will outweigh how much stuff you've accumulated or what job you ended up with. The idea is to be able to let go so much that in the end you can say to your body, thanks for the ride and still be smiling (without a pencil in your mouth).

It's our ability to regulate our attention, reduce our reactive nature and cultivate positive emotions, that points the way to health and happiness. If we can calmly observe our own habits of thinking clearly, we can see it in others and have greater empathy. Increasing the limited view of how we see our world and ourselves should be the next phase of human evolution; to extend the breadth of our consciousness and expand our range of choices. This will lead to appropriate alternatives and we'll be able to select each choice before we act on it. People who comprehend biological processes and make thoughtful choices shift from their self-centred world-view to a much larger interconnected whole.

They can become wise people; make choices and take actions that have long-term benefits for the future. The application of mindfulness will have an impact on social inequities, climate crisis, poverty and disease. I hope if nothing else we move to a world where it's not survival of the fittest but survival of the wisest.

Acknowledgements

I thank and kiss the ground before my friend and brilliant editor Joanna Bowen. Without her, this book would be an incomprehensible jumble of random and unfathomable thoughts and oddly spelled words. She put chaos into order.

My Professor of MBCT at Oxford University, Mark Williams for being such an inspiration and passing his wisdom along with Melanie Fennell and John Peacock.

Dr Mark Collins who saved me when I was deep in the darkness and Ros who always holds my hand when I'm down there.

Rowena Webb, my publisher at Hodder and Stoughton along with Maddy Price.

Thanks to Serge Seidlitz for his great illustrations.

To Michael Foster for setting all this up, my agent Robert Caskie along with Caroline Michel.

Andrew Dellis for his help with neuroscience.

Simon Whitesman for his help with mindfulness.

My family Ed, Maddy, Max and Marina for their constant supply of humour and endless supply of love.

My friends who stand by me.

My parents who made me.

My relatives in America (the Hambourgers) who got my parents out of Austria just in time, without which I would not be possible.

Thanks to authors

Jon Kabat-Zinn, Mark Williams, John Teasdale, Zindel Segal, Antonio Damasio, Robert M. Sapolsky, David Eagleman, Daniel Goleman, Thomas Metzinger, Eric R. Kandel, Richard J. Davidson, Rebecca Crane, Rick Hanson, V.S. Ramachandran, Norman Doidge, Louis Cozolino, Rita Carter, Mihaly Csikszentmihalyi, Steven Pinker, Richard Dawkins, Lewis Wolpert, David Brooks, Jared Diamond, Daniel Kahneman, Paul Gilbert, Sharon Begley, Steven Johnson, Sue Gerhardt, Peter Fonagy, David Rock, Robert Dunbar, Aaron T. Beck, John Bowlby, and many hundreds of others who's brains I've mined.

Text acknowledgements

'Autobiography in Five Short Chapters' by Portia Nelson. Taken from *There's A Hole In My Sidewalk: The Romance of Self Discovery*, Souvenir Press Ltd (2004)

'The Guest House' by Jalal al-Din Rumi, translated by Coleman Barks with John Moyne. Taken from *The Essential Rumi*, HarperOne (2004)